Managing Your Individual Computing Project

An Agile Approach for Students and Supervisors – 2nd Edition

KARL A. COX, PhD

ISBN-13: 978-1542778114

ISBN-10: 1542778115

DEDICATION

To all computing students about to embark upon their individual project.

CONTENTS

ACKNOWLEDGMENTS

My first thank you goes to the University of Brighton who fostered upon me many hours of project management teaching in 2009 when I began there. Initially, I was not keen to teach this strange textbook subject that differed much from my experiences but fortunately I stuck with it and this book is one of the results. My second thank you goes to my first office mate at Brighton, Dr Bob Hughes, who was and is the project management guru. He put me straight on so many things to do with project management, including agile, I can't begin to thank him enough. Also, I must thank Professor June Verner, my line manager at NICTA, co-director of a business consulting company with me and project management specialist for bringing me into the world of project management in the first place. I would also like to thank my colleague, Jane Challenger Gillitt, for encouraging our students so much in their projects. Finally, but most especially, I would like to thank my students who have heard me rant on about the pointlessness of much of the traditional project management approaches and wax lyrical about agile. I thank more so those students I have supervised through the years and are the reason this book has been written.

Author's Note on the Second Edition: this version of the book has revised a number of inconsistencies from the first edition, that despite best efforts still kept themselves in the final text. A few extra words, here and there, have been added as the thought came to me. Changes to the planning document content – not the functioning of the tools – has occurred. If you just bought the first edition, don't panic; not a great deal has changed technically and the software tool function remains exactly the same. Thank you for buying the book.

CHAPTER 1: INTRODUCTION

It's important to state up front what this book is about, what it sets out to do. Like all projects, it is sensible to determine how it can be viewed as a success when you get to the end. What can we say about the book at the end? Did it succeed? That's not easy to say if it isn't clear its intention from the beginning. So, here it is. In, and only in, the context of final year computing and MSc computing projects, this book has the following purposes:

1) To show why traditional waterfall project management techniques are of little value to a single-person student project.
2) To present an agile project management approach that engages the student's enthusiasm and is of value to the project in a number of ways:
   a. The planning process is made clear and it helps the student progress.
   b. The student learns to plan thoroughly for the short-term, act on that plan, review and commence again.
   c. The student learns from this process.
   d. The student manages the project far more effectively as a result.
3) The student *should* get a better mark because of the good use of this agile approach when compared against traditional planning.

This last point is a bone of contention in that it isn't guaranteed, but when we see that the traditional 'one-shot' waterfall approach to planning is inadequate and inappropriate, we should find the student project works better, and more quality is achieved, through the agile planning approach. This ought to equate to a better mark and most importantly, a far more satisfying experience.

A real way to run a successful project?

Final year students have a lot of things to contend with. The individual project is one of their bigger issues. There is a lot to take in and a lot of preparation to be done. In the world of student computing projects (that is, any project that revolves around or uses software or products of its lifecycle), it tends to be the case that a Gantt chart is produced at the start and is then ignored until the final write-up before submission. I have always found project management of this type to be very unrewarding for me as a supervisor but mostly for students, who could do a great deal more on their projects if they had the right tools and the right approach. There are three ways to manage student projects. The first is to not bother at all with any project management. The second is to follow a traditional planning approach where you plan the whole project in advance. The third way is to have a rough sketch of the wider project but plan in detail only for the next two weeks. The third way is the agile approach presented in this book.

In John Carroll's excellent book, *Agile Project Management*[1], he presents a diagram of the difference between traditional project

---

[1] John Carroll, *Agile Project Management,* InEasySteps Ltd, 2012.

management and agile project management. This diagram struck a strong chord and is reproduced, with my own amendments, in figure 1.1.

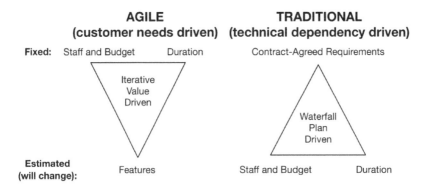

Figure 1.1. The upside down world of traditional management

On the right we see a "Traditional" triangle that has at the point one item that is fixed: the signed-off and sealed Contract-Agreed Requirements. At the fat bottom end there are two items that are estimated: Staff and Budget (the resources) and Duration (the length of the project in time units such as days or weeks or months). 'Estimated' means the original amounts, dates and people will change. Carroll compares this to the "Agile" inverted triangle (on the left) where there are two fixed elements: Resources (Staff and Budget) and Duration; the estimated element is the Features delivered (or the 'not contract-dependent' requirements). This means that not all features, or requirements, are likely to be delivered. It's possible they all will, but not probable. However, the most important requirements will be delivered, all being well on the project. The traditional approach to planning determines that *all* requirements have to be delivered – and more or less worked out at the very start – and then a plan-driven development can commence where money and people (resources) can be regularly evaluated and re-considered. As a manager, you'll ask the money people (probably the customer and/or sponsor), "Now we know a bit more about the complexity of some of these requirements, we need more time, we need more money and we need more people", otherwise the project is going to overrun in cost and time. In other words, the traditional planned approach to managing projects is as good as doomed before it gets going. This is because traditional planning automatically assumes the resources and time allocated to the project are going to be wrong from the outset and that you are always going to ask for more to deliver all the documented requirements. But what happens when there is no more time and no more money?

Agile on the other hand, being thoroughly fed up with the history of doomed projects, decided that it is not a good idea to overrun the project in terms of duration and resources but to set these as fixed (in that you know the budget cannot be blown; you know the staff needed for the project won't grow or shrink; you know the deadline *is* the deadline – it won't slip). Agile projects do not overrun nor do they overspend -- that's in principle! Agile focuses on delivery of what matters most to the customer, that is, what is most valuable *now*. So this means that not all features may be delivered within the time frame and budget for the project, but the most important features must be, and that is what matters most to customers: delivering the most valuable features first.

It does not take long to realise that the 'Agile triangle' naturally fits with the one-person student project. A student project has the following fixed elements: duration and resources. This means that what has to be estimated are the actual features. Some features do have to be delivered – such as project documents and a report of the student's experiences – to meet the university's requirements for an acceptable project. But the content of the products (be it software and/or technical documentation) can only be estimated at the outset.

This Book

This book presents an agile, simple, effective and informative approach for students who are undertaking a final year or Masters-level project. Particularly, this book is aimed at computing-oriented students – and their supervisors. There's no real need to go through the history of traditional and agile project management methodologies and principles though these will be discussed where necessary. There is, however, a need to go into some depth about student project characteristics and why an agile approach to project management fits and a traditional approach does not. This is not a philosophical discussion but a practical consideration based upon experience and common sense.

From the outset, the anticipated readers for this book are:

1. Students undertaking computing-oriented / software engineering / computer science / business computing / information systems / digital media development projects ('computing projects' for short, at undergraduate and masters level but not PhD).

2. Their supervisors.

If you are a supervisor or student who is already recommending or using an agile planning approach to projects, then well done; how successful has the approach been? No need to read further? It would be beneficial if you did because the book may reinforce a few points you missed or you may spot a few points I missed and let me know so I can improve this book! If you don't know a lot about agile planning or don't use it, then please keep reading.

This book is not for history students writing a dissertation. I have a history degree so I know what I'm talking about here. The book's focus is on computing projects for brevity. Now, there's no reason why the approaches discussed in the book cannot be used in other disciplines and other kinds of projects, but examples and discussions will revolve around computing projects. The assumption is also that these computing projects need to produce a technical deliverable such as a piece of working code, or a design or a set of business process models, not just an essay or dissertation. Of course, part of the main deliverable for a student computing project is a report documenting experiences, processes and methods used. These deliverables are all ably managed by the approach outlined in this book when the approach outlined in this book is ably followed.

What students have to deal with – and their supervisors too!

Final-year undergraduate students and masters students are faced with a daunting prospect: the individual project. Not that the idea of doing a project is so scary – students have done group projects and individual assignments before, some of even a semester's duration. What is most daunting is the fact that the final year project, or the masters project, has to be done alone outside the embrace of any other module, whose material informs the topic and specifics of the deliverable. The project is its own module (or unit), weighted typically at 40 credits, double the effort, expectation and outcome of a year-long taught module. For the masters student, the project is the difference between a post-graduate diploma and a masters qualification.

An undergraduate project is typically of one academic year's duration. This is, at least, the expectation. The work that goes into the project may not be a year's duration because students may take a few months to get up and running. It can be daunting: Just where do you begin on a year-long project? Some universities, including mine, attempt to prep the student to the task prior to arriving at the final year. There may be "how to do research" modules with an outcome of a project proposal and a brief literature survey. This is good in helping form the idea of the project and in turning the student's attention in the right direction. But it does not help the student in actually conducting the project other than find a topic and determine a vague set of deliverables. Most universities run the final year undergraduate project during the whole of the final year, whilst the student has to attend and pass other modules throughout. A few universities give their students the entire second semester of the final year to work on their projects, with no distractions from other modules (and with a higher credit emphasis of 60 credits rather than the standard 40 – meaning even higher expectations for a better deliverable). Masters students often get only 16-20 weeks to start, conduct and complete their project. In some instances they will have six months. Whatever the time frame, in all cases, time is of the essence. In all cases, project management is important. But in most cases I have seen, project management is treated as a bit of a joke. And I teach project management so I know what I am looking for and at. The reason I have come to this conclusion through my 20 years of practical experiences, research and discussion with my students and in supervising and marking many more projects on top of this, is that traditional, waterfall-oriented project management is entirely unsuited to a short, intense, one-person project. But why is this?

What's wrong with the traditional approach?

My experience of around 100 student projects (undergraduate and masters as a supervisor and marker) is there are four main problems that students encounter in their concept of what their project entails:

1) The student thinks the project is a challenge but in reality its scope is too small – not enough work has been defined at the start, leaving the student to flounder towards the middle and end or to not put anywhere near enough effort into it. An example of Parkinson's Law in practice: work expands to fill the time available.

2) The student thinks the project deliverables are accomplishable but in reality the project's scope is far too big – meaning there is simply too much to do in the time frame and so the student works flat out to cover all the requirements but does not put in the time to get the necessary quality across the board. Some things just don't get enough attention to be good enough quality and as a consequence are awarded poor marks.

3) The student just doesn't know whether the scope is too big or too small until close to the end of the project when it is too late.

4) The student's supervisor also is uncertain. He or she may have 5-10 project students in any one year. Keeping track of who is where with what is not straightforward. I, myself, have found it frustrating to see a lack of progress in students who can all do much better.

One reason why the above four points occur is because the tools that traditional project management recommends for students are wholly inappropriate. Tools such as calculation of effort estimates or of resource allocation, of dependency identification (and ensuing panic!) or of calculating the critical path are to the student of no value because they are designed for complex, long, multi-person projects (often of several years duration). A student project is none of these. The traditional focus is on long activities such as doing the whole design over several weeks, rather than on what is most valuable now to the student's customer (be the customer himself, his supervisor or external).

I spent time investigating why students struggle to produce high quality work in the right amounts and I have come to the inescapable conclusion that students are not managing their time well, are not setting realistically achievable daily, weekly and fortnightly tasks, and none of this is through any fault of their own. When it comes to preparing students for projects, we tend to focus on the production of a plan of action, a project plan for the entire project. This nearly always takes the form of a Gantt chart, the traditional project manager's tool for plotting the direction of a project. But there's a problem with this; well, several problems, actually.

There is an assumption that a Gantt chart is necessary for a project to succeed. But I've not found this to be the case on student projects. Why not? A Gantt chart needs to be completed up-front for the whole project yet things change on a project all the time, such as the customer's immediate needs. So the plan after week one is effectively wrong. Also, producing a plan for an entire project before much is known about the project, and then being held accountable to the story of that original plan, is foolish. Neither students nor supervisors are to blame. It's just been the way it has been and it's time to change.

What's in this book?

There's a better way to manage your project. It may look daunting to begin with but actually it is a lot easier for students to deal with even if they have to put a little more time into planning and reviewing than they might otherwise have done.

Chapter 2 will make a case for a move away from the Gantt chart approach, the traditional planning approach. In its place, I am proposing a much more appropriate Agile approach which is tailored for single-person projects of durations that fit student projects. This better approach puts forward the simple premise that planning the traditional way is built on assumptions that are entirely unsuited to a student project which has a fixed deadline, limited resources (in terms of people, just one is doing the work!) and must deliver high quality (high value) results. Some of the deliverables follow the structure set out by your university's requirements such as what the chapter headings should be, and some of the topics addressed, such as a reflective report. But also, there is a high degree of variability around what features / requirements / software / hardware / middleware / innovations / documentation and so on are produced.

Chapter 3 presents the agile tools that the student and supervisor will need to manage the project. The three tools are:

- Project Feature Backlog: a list of technical features and project deliverables including what release / iteration these features and deliverables may go in.

- Iteration Feature List: a highly detailed list of the deliverables, tasks and activities in a two-week iteration, including the effort estimates in hours for each task, and a place to daily record the effort actually done for each task.

- Burndown chart: documenting the current pace (velocity) of producing an iteration's features and products against ideal effort.

This may sound like a very short list but in actual fact pretty much all eventualities are covered. Risk is handled in the bi-weekly planning and reviews, and in the continual releases. Estimation comes into play in the iteration feature list. There's no need for a communication plan – this is written into each iteration plan on a weekly / bi-weekly cycle. Students should meet supervisors on a weekly basis or more so. If there's an external customer then the student will have to arrange how and when to meet and communicate with the customer.

Now that both approaches have been presented chapters 2 and 3, it's time to put them side by side and compare them directly. Chapter 4 takes a two-week iteration from the agile approach and compares it against a two-week period taken out of a Gantt chart from the traditional planning approach.

Chapter 5 considers the commitment and expectations of both the supervisor and customer in order to get the most out of this agile management approach.

No approach is perfect and the imperfections – or issues – that could arise and have arisen are presented in chapter 6. There are potential solutions or ways to consider addressing the issues and these are also presented.

Chapter 7 provides a summary and revisits key points made in the book.

On last thing to make your life a lot easier. I've put together an agile tool that runs on Microsoft's Excel for you to download that is used to provide the examples in the book. You can get it for free at: www.drkarlcox.com/agile -- just click on the 'Burndown' button to download it.

Let's now look more closely at why we need to move away from standard Gantt charts and traditional project management of student projects.

CHAPTER 2: THE TRADITIONAL 'WAY'

At the outset let me say that where projects are mainly manufacturing or engineering hardware and may involve only a small software aspect, then a traditional waterfall project management approach is most likely the best development lifecycle to use. However, for primarily software-oriented projects the waterfall approach is proven not to work well. But just exactly what is the traditional waterfall approach?

The Traditional Planning Approach

There is a complex, interrelated set of deliverables on a traditionally planned project and these are now described.

The Product / Work Breakdown Structure (almost the same but not quite) is a diagram that shows the project's intermediate and final products needed during the project (such as a database design or user acceptance tests). The idea is the manager can then work out what work needs to be done to make those products.

An Activity Network Diagram (almost isomorphic to a Gantt chart) shows the dependencies between the products in the work breakdown. It's isomorphic in the sense you can press a button in a leading project management software tool and it converts one diagram into the other. In some textbooks you see a Product Flow Diagram between the Work / Product Breakdown Structure and the Activity Network Diagram which helps in converting a Product Breakdown Structure into an Activity Network Diagram. There are also Product Descriptions that give "descriptions" of all products especially how they may be tested and what standards and quality they adhere to.

The Resource Allocation table or histogram indicates which person – a job role or named individual in reality – does what from the activity network diagram. A Gantt chart puts the resource allocation and activity network together into one picture.

A Risk table documents, if following Prince2 principles, all possible risks to the project, activities, resources and everything else. The table gives a basic idea of what to do about a risk if it is going to cost a lot and is more likely than not to arise during the project.

There are also Effort Estimation methodologies that take on one mathematical form or other. These are often called parametric tests; examples are Use Case Points, Function Points, COCOMO, COSMIC, estimation by analogy and no doubt there are others. Function Points are probably the most widely used and they work by guessing the size of a transaction (feature) using a formula by adding up inputs, entities employed and outputs and multiplying each using particular complexity weightings. The result is then calculated against productivity rates – how fast the average function point takes to programme on an average project. The productivity rate helps in working out the duration. Do this calculation for every transaction (or function), add all efforts together and you have an effort estimate for the project that can then be converted into a monetary figure for the project. All of this is done before the project really gets underway and before a whole lot is known about the project, the requirements or even the customer. As such, it is a pretty random affair but looks intelligent and professional. As one of my former professors once said in reference to parametric modelling: "You might as well look at sheep's entrails to get a better estimate!"

How is a student expected to do all this planning work for a project when he has little to no idea of what the project truly entails? Well, this is a bit of a problem. We ask students to produce at least a Gantt chart for the project but Gantt charts are really for projects with more than one resource. Gantt charts are suited to more than single-person projects. Figure 2.1 presents a Gantt chart created in Microsoft Excel. It's a plan for a whole project with lots of things going on at the same time. It is quite detailed as if the plan was devised by someone who knew everything that was going to happen and when. Though this is the whole point of traditional planning, having the plan itself is not going to help a lot other than point out to the student her project is not going to plan because within a week or two the schedule will be out. Is the student at this point expected to re-write the entire project plan only for that revised plan to be wrong by the end of the following week? This is what studious project managers do: keep re-writing the plan. For students, at this point it is simpler and easier to ignore the plan until the final write up starts, one or two weeks before the submission deadline.

In a way, the Gantt chart appears to be clear cut and every activity reasonable and well scheduled. For some projects this may well be all that is required for success but this is rare. The problems using a Gantt chart on a student project are:

1) When the student falls behind, or even if ahead of schedule, the whole Gantt chart has to be adjusted either forwards or backwards. So what is wrong with this? Perhaps nothing but then again perhaps there is something not right here. If you follow the iterative, agile approach, every two weeks there is a review when the student learns from his or her experiences in estimating activities and tasks and applies this knowledge to the next two weeks. This is an explicit activity whereas the Gantt chart just shifts and any explicit consideration of why the estimates were not in line with the actual experience is forgotten, if considered at all.

2) Are the planned tasks in the Gantt chart that are due to occur three or six months from now really going to occur to schedule? Perhaps they might, but it is really crystal ball gazing stuff. The agile world does not approach the future in blind hope. Apart from the immediate iteration and perhaps the next one, there are no hard plans put in place. This is explored further in the next chapter.

3) Though there is some detail in the Gantt chart in figure 2.1, is there enough detail? Are all the tasks defined to the point where any one task could be completed in a matter of hours without the need for

further examination and refinement? What work is needed to deliver the 'Interface Wireframes' or the 'Architectural design'? How do we estimate how long all the wireframes will take to design, show to the customer and get approval upon or make changes to ready for another round of approval, when we don't know how long even one will take?

4) A single block of work that may include wireframes, content mock ups and a site map might be scheduled for a week's duration. It is fine to indicate that these activities need to be completed during that week but how long is each one? Do we need to decompose them further? Is each activity really one week in duration each? Or is it a day? Or a few hours? Or several days? Where can we include in this Gantt chart our experience of designing a single wireframe screen and then readjust the rest of the estimate accordingly, if all we have to work with is one single block?

As we will see, when an iterative approach – an agile approach – is taken from the beginning the student will have to review the project on a two-weekly basis and then plan ahead but only for the next two weeks in detail. This may seem to be the same thing as re-writing the Gantt chart, but it isn't because a far more accurate, realistic and satisfying plan is being produced and followed in the iterative approach. But before we get there, let's take a look at one of the other problems with the traditional approach to planning.

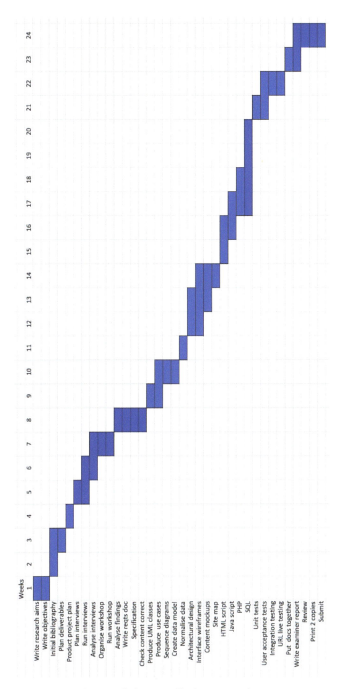

Figure 2.1. Detailed Gantt chart

The illusory big blocks approach

A significant illusory ability of the Gantt chart is to present big block activities as a way of masking and putting off the detail of what must be done or because the student simply does not know what must be done and is unaware of the finer details of the project. It's normal to be unaware of these details until the point where you need to consider the next step in the project. However, to remain unaware and to stick to just the big blocks throughout the project indicates the following:

1. The student does not know what to do.
2. The student doesn't care enough about having a plan.
3. The student realised that having a Gantt chart and using traditional project planning doesn't work on her project.
4. The supervisor is in the same boat as the student!

The big block Gantt chart consists of 4 main activities:

1. Requirements – which lasts about 4 weeks.
2. Design – which then follows for 6 weeks.
3. Coding – after all the design work, for 6 weeks.
4. Write up (of project) – which lasts for about 2 weeks.

There's normally about 4 weeks for putting a proposal together that would include some research work and hence there is no real plan at

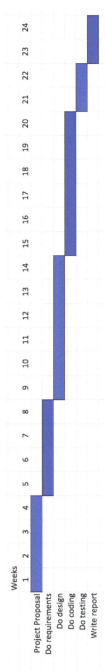

Figure 2.2. Big blocks Gantt chart

this point because the student does not feel the actual project has commenced yet but rather this first 4 weeks or so is just a warm up. It is understood students need time to define a project but they should be able to do this in week 1 or week 2 at the latest. They can use the agile tools presented in the next chapter to help them work out what is needed first. There's also a 2-week testing phase that may be added toward the end of the project. Whether it took two weeks to do is anyone's guess. The big block Gantt chart may look like figure 2.2.

Although the big blocks approach makes life a lot easier in terms of putting off what has to be done… "What are you doing on your project?", "I'm still working on requirements / design /code" etcetera, there is a problem: just what exactly is being done? And what exactly has been completed? And when is enough *enough*? And how do we know whatever has been done is any good or correct? Students can hide behind the Gantt chart solely because it allows a student to do so. Supervisors can do this too! On many an occasion I have asked my student where she is on her requirements work and then will receive a 20-bullet pointed list saying, "The system should do something." That's it for 4 weeks' work? Yes, it seems so. That requirements list could have been worked out in a day. This means almost 4 weeks of the project has delivered nothing and neither has the student learned much. Are we still on schedule? How do we know?

Many student projects have no project planning at all. So before you think I have thoroughly and unfairly condemned the Gantt chart, think again. At least the big blocks approach provides a visible document. It's almost better than nothing. Almost? Well, if there is no documentation, no documented plan, then there's nothing to hide behind that pretends the right effort and quality is being put into the right deliverables at the right time. There's nothing to use to obscure a lack of progress. If you're a PhD student you will be asked to produce a timeline for your work ahead over the next few years. Big blocks work in this context because the PhD student has been asked to produce a well-known formula. There's no real benefit to anyone. But the big blocks plan works in maintaining this illusion. It's hard to know exactly what you will be doing in two years from now. Time management is always a problem for PhD students – they are too focussed on the minutiae of detail and on the perfection they are trying to achieve. But that's PhD students – I know because I was one!

How does the traditional planning, be it the detailed Gantt or the big blocks approach make for a good undergraduate project? The student's goals are, most likely:

1.   Get a First class award.
2.   Build / design something cool.
3.   Learn something.
4.   Make it as easy as possible to achieve 1 above.

You could resolve the big blocks approach by including as much information as possible in the Gantt chart as in figure 2.1. But you are assuming you know the information before you get there. As you probably don't, you will end up guessing. And this will lead to the realisation that guesswork doesn't help a lot so you end up with the big blocks. Or you guess. Both of which are problematic. And then you leave the project planning as done and ignore it until your supervisor says something, or doesn't, as the case may be. It's all a bit unsatisfactory. On the surface traditional planning looks good but it has a lot of false assumptions especially for a one-person student project.

Saying all the above, it is ironically the case that when you are planning using the agile approach, you will make note of the big block activities and deliverables because they will be added to the project's main feature list, which will include all documentation, all sub-products (such as a data model) and end products such as an idea of the key functions and screens. A big blocks Gantt will go no further than acknowledge there is an activity to be done that leads to a deliverable, if the student has noted the actual deliverable too. There is no detail added whereas the agile approach almost forces the student to define the detail when it really needs definition for the 10-day iteration cycle.

False assumptions of traditional planning

Disclaimer: Before the reader thinks I am condemning traditional planning in all circumstances, I am only doing so in reference to a one-person student computing project of between 3 months and one year's duration and how illogical, it seems to me at least, it is to follow the heavyweight planning approach that is traditional waterfall planning. If you look at the statistics on how successful software projects have been historically, it is not very nice reading. With reported failure rates ranging from 35-85 per cent[2], and many of them following the process of traditional planning and management, then something must be wrong. How we have accepted failure as the norm is beyond my comprehension.

If we use the analogy of bridge building to make the point: a large and complex project of long duration and high cost. What if we apply the same failure rates from traditional IT projects to bridge building projects? It is reported regularly that nearly 50 per cent of IT projects fail to meet some of the customer's requirements, that anywhere between 30 and 70 per cent fail completely – and higher as we've just found out above. Are these figures acceptable in building bridges? What if we were commissioned to build a bridge across a ravine that had side by side dual carriageways on it so vehicles could go back and forth? If 50 per cent of these bridges delivered only one single lane going each way or only one way would this be successful? Or four lanes

---

[2] One large systems integration company in Asia I worked with confided they had an 85 per cent failure rate in their IT projects (which are admittedly large). This may sound an exceptionally high rate but such failure rates are not uncommon around the world, especially in government circles.

but only to half-way or three-quarters of the way across? We could not possibly view these as successful. If such project planning and management led to this level of failure so regularly, after 50 years of trying, the approach would have been abandoned years ago. But in IT failure is accepted far too lightly – it is a cultural norm.

The Agile revolution in computing projects is a direct reaction to this history of failure and frustration. Now firmly established in many organisations, Agile methods such as Scrum, Lean Development and Extreme Programming are leading to far more successful projects than previously, when the agile practices are properly applied. As I said earlier, it is not the purpose of this book to analyse different project management methodologies except where necessary and where practical, so I very much recommend that readers discover these Agile practices for themselves. There is plenty of material out there. This book will address what is needed for our purposes here only.

The traditional project manager's role and why it doesn't work

A traditional project management approach does not work well on student projects. It is not an easy task to be a project manager. I have worked with a few and been one myself. Not easy. Stressful. No fun. Premature balding. The list goes on.

The tools described above used for traditional project planning are developed primarily by one person, the project manager, and he will deploy these tools on a project where there's a lot of unknown work to do, with a lot of people doing it. Again, I turn to the exceptional book by John Carroll, *Agile Project Management*, for pointing out what had been staring me in the face… but I couldn't see it. Carroll explains that a traditional project manager on a multi-person project has to handle the following:

Responsibility: planning and all project work to the business and the customer. This means the project manager is responsible for the planning work and for negotiating and communicating with the customer and the business he is employed in. The manager has responsibility for the technical deliverables -- but why should the project manager be responsible for the quality of programme code? Isn't that the role of the programmer? How can a project manager accurately estimate the effort needed for coding the solution before any code commences?

Control: schedule, budget, estimates, risks, resources. All those planning products have not only to be created but managed. Some are really hard to do. Some you may have your hands tied already for instance, if a budget has been allocated and it is fixed; you'll never get more money no matter what you try. So when the project runs out of money – as any good manager would have figured out a while ago – then the project manager is made responsible for this and held to account. But why should it be the manager's responsibility to control spending if the manager did not set the budget?

Authority: for everything. The manager should not have authority over technical matters he knows little about. This authority should lie with the technical people. Yet it is presumed the manager has the power to do almost whatever he sees fit. Managers plan the project, set the tasks, allocate the work and await the outcome. Thankfully most managers do not exercise their right to cut code or act as the user in acceptance testing, but it is presumed they could do so given they have the authority. When project managers do decide to join their team in the development work, you know the project is going to struggle. There have been cases of allocating the business analyst project management responsibilities also. This means neither job gets done well.

All this responsibility, control and authority is an awful strain on one person. Project managers get paid well but they also get fired a lot, too. So to put this load on to a student is a bit over the top. Yes, on a one-person project, the student has to take ownership, control, responsibility and authority for the entire project. But the fact that we would expect such heavyweight management for a student project seems to be a step too far. Though we don't wish to promote hacking or chaos, we don't want to implement a full-scale Software Engineering Institute-style personal software process on our students. There are better ways.

How the false assumptions of traditional planning affect student projects

If we take on the assumptions of traditional planning in our student projects, we falsely assume:

All requirements are known up-front and won't change. Yet we all know this to be a false statement. Not all requirements will be known and even in the rare cases they are known, they will most likely change. We push our students to plan around a set of unknown requirements that were elicited from a customer the student has only met once or twice. We then plan the entire project out of thin air. Perhaps it was possible to get all requirements (business, user and technical) prior to anything else happening on a project but this today is unlikely because of the ability to rapidly produce a prototype or a working segment of code. So when a few requirements are known, it's natural the student wants to get these into working code or a prototype as quickly as possible. Students should be encouraged to do so because it breeds confidence when they find out they really can code. And in any case, requirements change. Added to this, many (if not all) students are not keen on documentation until it is an absolute necessity.

We falsely assume: The student will design the entire system first before any code is cut. We assume he or she will produce a complete design: entities, objects and so on because we believe we have all the requirements. No code is cut until all of the design is approved. How can we approve all the design if none of it has been tested by code? All we can say is that it maybe, might work. Maybe.

We falsely assume: The student will code the entire system in one go. Though it is possible to code an entire system in one go, it is really unlikely this will be a good approach unless the system is a very small prototype. The false assumption that all the design is correct and unchanging because all the requirements are correct and unchanging springs to mind.

We falsely assume: The entire software product will work with little-to-no testing. Is it realistic to leave tests until the end? Is it realistic to assume students will put a massive effort into testing? Will every line of code compile without error? Will each implemented function return a correct result? Will all attempts to crash a function fail? Will none of the by now spaghetti code need to be simplified and the solution streamlined (refactored)? Will the requirements remain a constant throughout the project? Will the design guide the coding perfectly? Are you getting the point yet? If you can honestly answer "yes" to every question then stop reading here.

We hope the customer will remember who her student is after four months with no contact! Personally, I encourage my students to spend as much time with their customer as possible, to become part of their furniture, so long as the student remembers she is still a university student! Now if the student does not have a customer this is a different story but if we assume she does, then the more the student learns about the customer's business the greater the chance of a successful project. But if we stick to the traditional disengagement approach of a waterfall method where we spend the early part of the project working out requirements but post this have little communication with the customer, the project and student will struggle. The student may be buried away on his project working on designs and code but will the customer want those solutions when her business has changed without the student being aware of it? Will the customer remember what she wanted four months after their last contact when the student asks for a glowing letter of commendation that can be quoted in his project report?

We falsely assume: The student will follow the Gantt chart to the letter. I regularly ask students where they are in their plan, their Gantt chart. I elicit a typical response along the lines of: "I'm doing design now. It will be finished in six weeks." OK, I would say, good news, progress. But, as stated above, is it really progress or an excuse to not do any work (both for the student *and* supervisor)? It is assumed that a linear process of construction / examination is adopted until the final report is submitted for marking. There is a false assumption that students will work in a straight line and do not jump from one task to another. It is falsely assumed that a student will not work on a task that is dependent upon another even though that other task has not yet been completed – or started.

We falsely assume: The student (and supervisor) will remember there is a Gantt chart! It's inevitable a student will forget the Gantt chart because her supervisor will too. Whether the big block approach or the minutiae of detail approach is taken, both parties will forget it. Why is this? There are many reasons:

- Because the deliverables will be few and far between.

- Or because the Gantt chart is so inaccurate by this time (week 2 of the project onwards!) that the work occurring isn't where the Gantt chart is.

- Or the plan's content is wrong because the project changed but the chart didn't.

A Gantt chart is a poor way to monitor progress and we will return to this point later because it is a driving force behind changing the approach.

We falsely assume: The student will produce a risk table to start with and if not will be asked to produce one early into the project. A traditional planning approach assumes the student will address all conceivable risks at the start of the project and document them in a risk table, and then manage them throughout. But to assume this is foolish because given little is known about the project at the start, how can we assume anything concrete about the risks?

We falsely assume: The student will monitor and manage risks throughout. Given that a lot of project managers do not do this, we cannot expect students to do this either. Don't blame managers for this. Risk management is a whole project by itself. The manager and project have enough to be getting on with. So long as the show stoppers are dealt with, then the remaining risks will probably be ignored until they occur, if they occur. This is not to say that ignorance is the right way to deal with risks, but it is the common way to do so. However, I do agree wholeheartedly with the agile approach that business risk is managed by the customer, and technical risks – where appropriate – are managed by the technical people.

I've heard the following risk advice given to students and given it myself. It amounts to just one item: encouraging the student to back up their work at multiple locations. And provided the student actually backs up her project work in two or three different locations, one of them on her university's or customer's server, then that's enough for risk.

It is falsely assumed equal time is given to the project per week (there are no other distractions for the duration of the project). Students have other weekly commitments such as assignments and exams to deal with. Plus they have a life. There is part-time work and there are periods of vegetation followed by bursts of activity. The assumption of a repeated set weekly effort[3] is entirely unrealistic. So to

---

[3] For the sake of argument, let us assume a project is 400 hours-worth of work to get 40 credits. Given two semesters of 12 weeks duration (24 weeks), if we divide 400 by 24 we get just over 16. So we should expect 16 hours work on the project every week or 32 hours every 10 working days. That's just over three hours per work day.

big-block plan is also entirely unrealistic. A student may work for 40 hours in one week and nothing in the preceding and following two! Unlike an office environment, there is no control of hours for a student other than when he or she is supposed to be in classes. When we get to the next chapter you will see that we do hope to reverse this trend somewhat and ask the student to put in regular hours – so we can estimate effort per task more accurately – but as said, it is unlikely there will be much consistency in hours worked when it comes to assignment submission weeks. My experience shows this to be the case with the agile approach – there is in fact greater consistency of regular effort because the tool makes it very plain how much work the student didn't do.

We assume that a student will have regular meetings with the supervisor throughout: once a week, on the same day of the week, at the same time and of the same duration. This is an ideal and in my experience has rarely happened. Staff are allocated 30 minutes per student per week on my employer's workload model. If I have 8 students per academic year that is 4 hours work per week. There were weeks when under a traditional management approach I didn't see my students. Then there were short bursts of meetings every couple of days. Then a gap. Then more meetings. I am being honest here. Perhaps my colleagues meet students every week no matter what. I don't waste time meeting if there is nothing to meet about. I assume my students work consistently on their project whereas the reality is they don't. So scheduling to meet regularly is a good idea but a poor practice under a traditional approach. An agile approach is different in that there are joint planning and review meetings every week. I discuss this in chapter 5 when I describe the responsibilities of the supervisor. To be successful with agile, the business has to change as well as the IT and it is no different here in a university setting.

Traditional waterfall management dictates that the critical path is key. Traditional planning calls for the manager to work out the longest pathway through a set of dependent activities that when followed will produce your product. This longest pathway has no float, meaning no degree of freedom to delay starting work on any activity on its path without extending the duration of the project. So if we ask our students to take this traditional path to management we ask them to be very careful about looking after this so-called critical path. But does this make sense? What if the activities that look the longest on the Gantt chart actually were not all of highest value to the customer (be it the student, supervisor or a third party)? What if some other activities were important to get done first, were of higher priority but not on the critical path because of their shorter length? Does traditional planning document atomic items such as individual requirements or user stories as activities? Religious observance to the critical path is a pathway of false hope. A student needs to deliver what will bring greatest value not only to herself but to her customer. By holding solely to the longest thread of activities, it is likely that not enough thought has gone into priorities. The big blocks critical path (and the entire plan) follows the well-trodden path of high risk: gather, analyse and document all requirements, get them approved, only then create all the design, only then write all the code, and only then conduct whatever testing the student has time for. Traditional planning assumes all activities on the critical path are of equal priority. What about other activities not on that critical path yet rated with the same Must Have priority? The critical path is calculated as a duration event not as a priority event. Obviously, some technical work must be done in order for the priority features to be developed and function but do students need to do all the underlying technical work before commencing on the feature development just because that technical work is on the critical path?

It is also falsely assumed that the student's project goals / aims are fixed. Once an initial proposal for the project has been submitted and approved, we as supervisors may hold students to their original idea, goal or aim. But the student may have changed direction for many reasons such as a lack of skill in a specific area, or the realisation that the project topic is not what the student really wants to do or likes, or the student's customer having a significant degree of uncertainty. So goals that are very general: "demonstrate skill in programming in C#" or to "model a set of business processes" are not precise enough to be of any substantive meaning to the student or the supervisor. More precision and refinement will be required. It is the case that a lot of project aims are not decided until the end of the project! I, for one, found this to be the case when finishing my PhD – just what was it about? I couldn't articulate a precise goal and aim until I'd done the work. The rough aims changed as I progressed. So it should be with a student's final year or MSc project (and with PhDs!).

One last point reiterated because it matters:

We falsely assume: A student's customer will really love the 'product' without having seen it or the student for a very long time! The rich and bountiful feedback a student will want from her customer may not be quite so forthcoming as anticipated in the traditional project process. Lack of contact means lack of feedback. An agile approach would mean on-going continual engagement.

In reality student projects are different from the perception

In reality, aims and requirements are always in flux early because of uncertainty about the student deliverable and even the project area.

In reality, students work in bursts of activity surrounded by bouts of inactivity as other priorities take centre stage. Despite our best intentions, we cannot convince all students to address the project as a full-time or even part-time job.

In reality, more time is really needed with the supervisor early in the project as ideas form and requirements move from none to abstract to more concrete. More hours should be scheduled early in a project in order to get the student up-and-running much faster. Even if these are thrice-weekly 15-minute stand-up meetings for the first six weeks, this would be enormously beneficial. Direction changes so rapidly early on in a project as some things become clearer and others more mysterious. But only spending a maximum of 30 minutes a week in a solitary meeting means that any uncertainty and confusion only gets formally addressed once a week. This is not enough. Students need more time up-front in order to get their project really off the ground.

What a student project looks like

There are a number of classic characteristics of a student project that fit the idea of agile management far more than traditional. Some of these characteristics are fixed and some are variable.

The student project consists of the following **fixed** components:

One developer (the student!). Though it is possible to have two students working on a single product, in effect there is only one person per project. A traditional project management plan is devised around working out the number of staff who would deliver the ideal plan. Agile projects have more or less fixed team sizes.

Fixed deadline. Students get no flexibility to delay their submission. If it is late it is marked as late and capped at 40 per cent (or 50 per cent for postgraduates). Agile projects work towards a fixed deadline. Each iteration is fixed in length. Traditional project management works toward calculating how long it will take to deliver all requirements, meaning the deadline is in flux.

Fixed cost (there is none allocated!). There's no point estimating cost as students normally are not permitted to charge like a consultant might.

Scheduled time with supervisor (30 minutes per week). Technically students are allocated a fixed meeting duration with staff per week in the staff workload model. This will vary in practice but this is the allocation. The student knows that meetings have time limits so they must prioritise what they want to discuss. So must supervisors.

Report deliverable for marking. Students will fail if there is no report submitted even if the product built is brilliant.

The student project consists of the following **variable** components:

Customer (external to university or within). A number of student projects involve a third party customer beyond the supervisor and the student. Students need a way to maximise time with their customer, to be the most efficient they can. A big block Gantt chart does not offer much opportunity for this but a two-week iteration that the agile approach takes does because fine details can be considered, and schedules can be moved about to fit the customer's schedule also.

Individual deliverables within the final submitted report. Obviously, the content of the report, that is, the requirements, vary based upon the project context. The technical deliverable will include whatever the student can get done in the time frame. There's no need to deliver all the requirements of the product as originally listed at the beginning of the project. This is contrary to the ideal of traditional project management but suits agile development perfectly. Only the most valuable requirements must be delivered.

Effort per week changes dependent upon other deliverables such as other assignments on the student's degree programme (this is known in advance because deadline dates should be announced at the start of the year or when the assignment is handed out). Students can easily flag the days they are scheduling to work on other activities, assignments or revision. This is reflected well in any two-week iteration plan. On the big block Gantt chart, it's hard to see exactly what's going on. In a detailed Gantt, like in figure 2.1, it's difficult to spot and means another rewriting of the plan.

The better way

There is a much more sensible and effective way to plan and manage a student project. The next chapter describes a very cut-down version of agile that isn't Scrum, it isn't DSDM, it isn't XP, it isn't even Lean. It's just what is needed. Let's take a look in chapter 3.

CHAPTER 3: AN AGILE SOLUTION

The reasons why we should move away from the traditional planning approach were explained in the previous chapter. We are now entering the realms of agile project management. Agile recognises that it is almost impossible to predict the future with any degree of accuracy. Often predictions are wildly wrong. So the point of taking the agile path is not even to try to do that. We won't plan out the whole project right at its beginning. We recognise that some specific deliverables have to be submitted by certain dates so we make a note of these and work towards them. But we won't write into a plan that six months from now we need to produce the code. With any luck, given a project that needs some code work done, we should be coding a lot sooner than that.

Instead, we will have a very rough idea of what the product might look like and do, making note of what those things may be in the *project feature backlog*. We then plan in detail for the immediate two weeks ahead only, writing the fine-grained activities we will conduct on an *iteration feature list*. From this we will deduce how quickly we are progressing visually against an 'ideal' or constant velocity of hours worked per day, our rate of progress, over those two weeks. That's called a *burndown chart*. When the two weeks are up, the supervisor and student review the progress made. Upon checking the project feature backlog for the major elements of the project, the student produces a fine-grained plan of action for the next two weeks. The student and supervisor (for the first iteration) decide how long each task may take in hours, make a note of this and compare against actual times taken to perform similar tasks in the prior iteration. This way if a similar task appears later in the project, the actual time taken to complete that task last time can be used as the estimate for how long it should take to do it this iteration.

This chapter will explore in detail three tools: the project feature backlog, the iteration feature list and the burndown chart. We will also examine the agile process of iteration. These three tools are quite simple to use and they are the only management tools you need for your project. They cover all eventualities, just about. Let's get into the detail now of the first tool you will use.

Project feature backlog

The project feature backlog is a table where all the major deliverables are placed for the entire project, and major tasks and activities the student will need to do along the way. In essence it is like that Gantt chart in figure 2.1 but there's no graphic involved. It's just a list. When the student begins the project, there's not a lot of idea as to what is needed. The student knows there are two reports, one a reflective report for examiners, and one representing the project deliverables such as models, designs, screens, code, test scripts and so on. Deliverables get added to the project feature backlog. Early deliverables such as the project proposal are added also. It's a high-level view of the things a student needs to produce. As new features are thought of, they are added. But it is more than just a shopping list.

The project feature backlog also contains columns headed: Priority, Planned Iteration, Actual Iteration, Total Planned Effort, Actual Planned Effort and whether the item is Complete? There's also the 'Log' heading where students can make a note of any issue or experience they had with that particular feature. This eliminates the log book as a separate deliverable and ties the recording of such experiences directly to the feature involved at the time it occurred. So there's no need to delve into the memory bank to try to remember just what the problem was with that function call two months ago. The student can note immediately what it is, as it is happening.

Figure 3.1 presents an outline of what the project feature backlog looks like. It's a spreadsheet and that's all you need. Note that features are boxed into iterations. As you can see, iterations 1 and 2 are planned, but none has occurred. The student is at the point of conducting the first iteration. The tasks and deliverables not boxed in with a thick line are the ones that have yet to be fully scheduled. Though they are assigned an iteration number, this is very flexible, dependent upon the immediate needs of the customer and the project. Note that iteration 1 contains the project brief and iteration 2 the project proposal report. These should be very short documents. The first at most a page that outlines the general idea of the project with key deliverables. The goal is to get this completed by the end of the second teaching week.

ID	Feature / Task / Deliverable	Priority	Planned Iteration	Actual Iteration	Total Planned Effort	Total Actual Effort	Complete?	Issues / Log
1	Iteration Planning	Must	1		3	0	N	
2	Project Scope Analysis	Must	1		16	0	N	
3	Project Brief Report	Must	1		6	0	N	
4	Iteration Review	Must	1		7	0	N	
1	Iteration Planning	Must	2		3	0	N	
6	Interview Customers	Must	2		18	0	N	
7	Project Proposal Report	Must	2		8	0	N	
4	Iteration Review	Must	2		3	0	N	
	Process modelling	Must	3					
	User stories and requirements document	Must	3,4					
	Strategic Modelling	Could	4					
	Data models	Must	5					
	Prototypes	Must	3 through 10					
	C# ASP.Net	Must	3 though 11					
	SQL database?	Should	?					
	Mobile version required?	Should	?					
	Examiner's report	Must	11, 12					
	Project documents	Must	11, 12					

Figure 3.1. Project feature backlog (Iteration 1, day 0)

Another key goal is the submission of the project proposal report as soon as possible so that the university's administrative deliverables don't get in the way of the work of the project itself for too long. Each item in the project feature backlog should have a rough estimate of hours to complete it so that 32 hours can be assigned to each iteration. A project worth 40 credits is in theory equivalent to 400 hours of work. That's roughly 16 hours per week term time, or 32 hours every iteration. Each iteration begins with a planning day and ends with a review day. These are vital and more about these key activities will be revealed later in this chapter.

Note that the activities listed in figure 3.1 are general sets of activities. Each is prioritised, as either Must have, Should have or Could have. This prioritisation is general in the sense that once each feature is decomposed into its specific parts in the iteration feature list, some parts of it may not be Must have even though overall it is considered as such. So the student should be careful when prioritising not to presume that all aspects of a feature, be it a document, a design or a functioning item of code exclusively be Must have or Should have or Could have. It is also the case that some features will receive a Won't have prioritisation but we will discuss this topic a little later.

When submitting the project proposal, it makes good sense to include within it the project feature backlog and, if done, an example iteration feature list and burndown chart. Supervisors and second readers expect to see some planning documents immediately. But be warned: you may find the second reader only knows about Gantt charts and may view your submission dimly. Please take the time to explain its meaning and please do not be put off by those who do not immediately understand your submission.

As each item in the project feature backlog needs to be addressed, it is placed into an iteration feature list. The item's specific elements are represented by breaking down the feature into much finer grained detail. This means that the single item in the project feature backlog represents the compilation of broken down tasks in the iteration feature list. As an example, let's take the first item in figure 3.1, 'Iteration Planning'. Total planned effort is 3 hours. It is prioritised as 'Must Have'. In the iteration feature list (figure 3.2), this single task of 'Iteration Planning' is decomposed into two smaller tasks:

1.1.   'Plan with supervisor', estimated as 1 hour's effort and a Must have.

1.2   'Detailed planning on own', estimated as 2 hours, also a Must have.

So the project feature backlog adds the combined estimated effort of 1.1 and 1.2 and places it in its table, which is 1 hour plus 2 hours, making 3 hours estimated effort for the planning task. You can record the combined actual effort here also, as well as whether another iteration is needed for the task at hand. Look at the second task in figure 3.1, 'project scope analysis', and you can see how those allocated

16 hours are decomposed into six separate tasks in the iteration feature list.

The project feature backlog is simply a general list so you and your supervisor – and customer – can keep track of the overall project progress. Are you more or less on target in terms of key features, key deliverables? What features – more or less – are you planning in the next iteration or two? It's important not to lose sight of the bigger picture so it matters that the project feature backlog is kept current. As a project progresses it is easy for students to get bogged down in a technical aspect and forget about recording progress and keeping planning current.

It is a discipline to do so and one worth learning now. This practice gets easier as the student learns, and maintaining it through the project becomes a lot easier. It will stand all students in good stead as they move on to their professional careers by taking such a professional attitude with them.

It's also the case that in some institutions a record is needed of contact between student and supervisor, to ensure all students and their supervisors are engaging in the project. The project feature backlog can act as this because the supervisor can sign off on either the planned iteration or the completion of it. Whether this is done at the project level or at the specific iteration level is down to the supervisor and student to decide. My experience is that supervisors need to be aware of the bigger picture more than the fine-grained detail. The supervisor needs to keep the student on track in hitting the project deliverable targets and on delivering the Must Have features. The supervisor also plays a vital role in overseeing the activity selection in the iterations but ultimately the student has to know the details herself, and discuss with the supervisor why each detailed feature is in each iteration and especially the effort assigned to it. Responsibility, however, lies with the student. The supervisor has authority to question, recommend changes and approve tasks but it is the student who does the detailed work, so it is her task to determine what should be done in each iteration, although at the approval and guidance of her supervisor and customer. Let's look at this core iteration planning and monitoring tool in detail now.

The Iteration Feature List

We begin with the iteration feature list[4] rather than the burndown chart because the burndown solely represents <u>visually</u> the current state of play with any particular iteration. The iteration is determined by the selection of appropriate features to address in that two week block. This decision is made by the student and the supervisor, at least in an advisory role. The customer, should there be one, also has a key role to play in determining the order of which features should be produced.

---

[4] Note that the burndown chart was created using the instructions provided at http://www.techbudha.com/2012/09/create-burn-down-chart-using-excel-in.html

It is important the student listen to the customer to get this right but at the same time keep in mind what is needed and when in order to progress. Here the supervisor needs to be up-to-speed on the dates that the university requires a submission and ensure that whatever is needed is put into the schedule for the right iteration, giving enough time to produce the submission. The earlier submissions on a project should be used as mere stage gates that have to be approved with yes/no. This may sound like sacrilege for some who are stuck on process and box-ticking. But the priority has to be given to producing the product at the end of the project, be it code or documents or both. In real projects, you don't get any reward for the planning documents. It's the code that counts. Time taken out to fulfil unnecessary university requirements such as producing an in-depth literature review take massive time out of the doing part of the project. Some reading (and documenting a bibliography) is required in order to ground the project, conduct research in new techniques or languages and aid in delivering the product; it is important this gets done. But projects should not be about delivering a discursive literature review. This sort of research is best served in other modules or units or at PhD level. The single-person student project (undergraduate and masters level) should really only be about producing a technical product to showcase the skills the student has learned. The reflective report is the place for any necessary references to back up experiences and outcomes, and for problem solving, and nothing else. Students need to be able to *practice* their skills and demonstrate this through realistic application.

Iteration 1 / Deliverable	Task	Priority	Task ID	Estimate Effort hours	Week 1					Week 2					Actual effort per task
					Mon	Tues	Wed	Thur	Fri	Mon	Tues	Wed	Thur	Fri	
1. Iteration Planning	Plan with supervisor/customer	Must	1.1	1	0	0	0	0	0	0	0	0	0	0	0
	Detailed planning on own	Must	1.2	2	0	0	0	0	0	0	0	0	0	0	0
2. Project Scope Analysis	Determine project scope	Must	2.1	6	0	0	0	0	0	0	0	0	0	0	0
	Customer analysis	Must	2.2	4	0	0	0	0	0	0	0	0	0	0	0
	Competitor analysis	Should	2.3	2	0	0	0	0	0	0	0	0	0	0	0
	Review project scope	Must	2.4	2	0	0	0	0	0	0	0	0	0	0	0
	Examine high likelihood risks	Should	2.5	1	0	0	0	0	0	0	0	0	0	0	0
	Review options for decisions	Should	2.6	1	0	0	0	0	0	0	0	0	0	0	0
3. Brief	Write Report Brief	Must	3.1	6	0	0	0	0	0	0	0	0	0	0	0
4. Iteration Review	Quality Review	Must	4.1	4	0	0	0	0	0	0	0	0	0	0	0
	Sign off	Must	4.2	1	0	0	0	0	0	0	0	0	0	0	0
	Review iteration	Must	4.3	2	0	0	0	0	0	0	0	0	0	0	0
Ideal - remaining work effort in ideal hours				32	29	26	22	19	16	13	10	6	3	0	
Actual - remaining effort in ideal hours				32	32	32	32	32	32	32	32	32	32	32	

3rd Oct 2016 - 16th Oct 2016

Figure 3.2. Feature List Iteration 1 Day 0

Employers want intelligent students who can *do* the job, not solely write a summary of what others have to say about it.

To demonstrate the iterative feature list let us take an example and explain it. You will see the basic feature list for iteration 1 in figure 3.2. at the very beginning before the iteration has commenced. All we have is the detail of the tasks and the estimates of hours needed per task, assuming the student needs to put in about 16 hours per week to keep up with the project workload. Again, estimation is a rough guide only but will be improved as the student progresses on the project, learning about the tasks and completing them. At this point, iterations ahead of the now can make use of the actual hours spent on tasks in order to get the later estimates more accurate. As can be seen from figure 3.2, each task that was listed in the project feature backlog for iteration 1 has been broken down into several steps, except for the Project Report Brief which is too small a deliverable to decompose further.

Note that the fourth activity, Iteration Review, has been allocated seven hours. This seems to be a lot of time for a review but in this case, a supervisor should be cautious to ensure the student is getting off to the right start and with the right quality immediately. So if more time is planned in the first iteration for review of progress and quality, this is acceptable. This amount of review time may not continue past this one iteration. Note that reviewing is not the same as testing. When code needs testing, it is a separate entry.

Agile often suggests that one day be allocated for the review. This should be the case from the second iteration onwards to the end of the project. One or two iterations before the final iteration – the report writing phase, typically – it is important to plan out what needs to be done to maintain the highest quality in delivering the final product for the customer and the project documents needed for assessment, and to allow for feedback on whatever may require the consideration of the customer and / or the supervisor.

The burndown chart

At this point it is important to introduce the visual graphic that will show the ideal daily effort to be made and compare it against the actual effort made. Before we get to examining how near or far away a student is from the ideal velocity – the recommended speed of which the student should travel to reach the destination on time – let's discuss velocity itself.

The idea of velocity is simple. At what constant speed should we ideally travel on a project in order to get the scheduled work done? Our iteration schedule is one iteration every two weeks, or a 10-day cycle. So we are setting out to travel ten days' worth of work each time. In figure 3.3 this is seen as the diagonal line. This line should remain straight for every iteration. There may be days of inactivity by the student and there will be public holidays but in terms of our planning ideal, the velocity should remain a constant. This allows us to see where

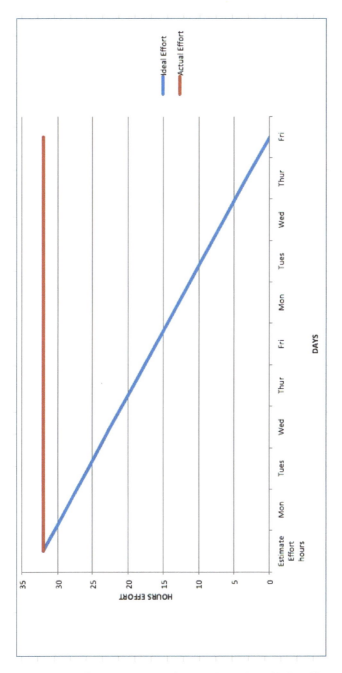

Figure 3.3. Burndown chart at iteration kick-off

we are going astray and bring us back on to the right path quickly because the other line will map our actual effort. The goal of each iteration is to have perfect estimates, where the actual effort matches the ideal, so that the actual effort line is exactly on top of the ideal; that is, the student's actual velocity matches the ideal velocity. Of course, this is not very likely, nor should we expect it to be. It's a guide and we should accept at the outset the ideal and actual may not align that closely, especially at the beginning of the project. But given a couple of iterations, things should change and we should see a closer ideal estimate to the actual effort because we can employ prior knowledge from previous iterations to estimate the next iteration's effort per task. In an ideal world estimates of effort should exactly match the real effort put into a project, and are not widely inaccurate as they currently are, we should be able to estimate every task equally.

This is the ideal where each activity has the same duration, no matter what it is, provided that the activity has been broken down into the lowest sensible level of detail. In this situation, the same effort should be employed on every feature or requirement or document and as such the same time should be taken to complete it. Still ideally, the two-week period of work should set a number of tasks that can receive the same effort every time. In practice, none of this is likely. It is most likely impossible, actually.

Given the history of estimation on software projects, which has been close to disastrous over the decades, because of the high degree of unknowns when estimates have to be made and the fact that focus has often been on things like lines of code or number of entities used per function call for a transaction, none of which considers the coder or the designer and what he or she can actually do, and the fact that each individual works at their own pace. This is why the student should make their own estimates, in collaboration with his or her supervisor, and revise these estimates as effort is applied to the project. Only through documenting the actual effort in the iteration feature list table, can anything sensible be learned from estimation. The estimation old order has changed and it is time to yield to the new, which was really obvious all along. So it is very important to plot actual progress against ideal progress. A simple chart is used to show this. Figure 3.3 shows the two lines plotted before any work has been done at the start of the iteration. The figure provides the graph for iteration 1, day zero. The horizontal line is actual effort. In this case, nothing has been done.

Let's move ahead now to day 2 on iteration 1. The idea for explaining how these tools work is to show the differences in the table and the graph every two days, and to explain that which needs explanation. Take a look at figure 3.4 of the iteration feature list. You will see that on days Monday and Tuesday of week 1, some effort has been made on planning and on the project scope analysis. The estimate of meeting the supervisor is one hour but only 30 minutes transpired. Another meeting should occur in week two (in reviewing the iteration) of this iteration so that missing half an hour can be made up the following week.

Iteration 1	3rd Oct 2016 - 16th Oct 2016				Week 1					Week 2					Actual effort per task
User Story/ Requirement / Feature / Deliverable	Task	Priority	Task ID	Estimate Effort hours	Mon	Tues	Wed	Thur	Fri	Mon	Tues	Wed	Thur	Fri	
1. Iteration Planning	Plan with supervisor/customer	Must	1.1	1	0.5	0	0	0	0	0	0	0	0	0	0.5
	Detailed planning on own	Must	1.2	2	1	1	0	0	0	0	0	0	0	0	2
	Determine project scope	Must	2.1	6	0	2	0	0	0	0	0	0	0	0	2
2. Project Scope Analysis	Customer analysis	Must	2.2	4	0	0	0	0	0	0	0	0	0	0	0
	Competitor analysis	Should	2.3	2	0	0	0	0	0	0	0	0	0	0	0
	Review project scope	Must	2.4	2	0	0	0	0	0	0	0	0	0	0	0
	Examine high likelihood risks	Should	2.5	1	0	0	0	0	0	0	0	0	0	0	0
	Review options for decisions	Should	2.6	1	0	0	0	0	0	0	0	0	0	0	0
3. Brief	Write Report Brief	Must	3.1	6	0	0	0	0	0	0	0	0	0	0	0
4. Iteration Review	Quality Review	Must	4.1	4	0	0	0	0	0	0	0	0	0	0	0
	Sign off	Must	4.2	1	0	0	0	0	0	0	0	0	0	0	0
	Review iteration	Must	4.3	2	0	0	0	0	0	0	0	0	0	0	0
Ideal - remaining work effort in ideal hours				32	29	26	22	19	16	13	10	6	3	0	
Actual - remaining effort in ideal hours				32	30.5	27.5	27.5	27.5	27.5	27.5	27.5	27.5	27.5	27.5	

Figure 3.4. Day 2 feature list

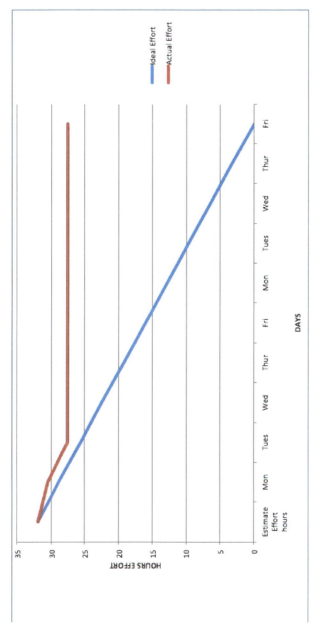

Figure 3.5. Day 2 burndown

This is a minor change in the table but a noticeable change in the burndown chart as shown in figure 3.5. As can be seen, the 'actual' line is no longer flat but has had some diagonal movement. From Day 3 onwards it is still a flat line because these days are yet to come. The actual effort is less than the ideal and as such it sits **above** the ideal line. It's a simple but expressive tool to show how much effort the student is putting in and combined with the feature list, this is all a student needs on a daily basis to manage the project, provided the feature list is kept up-to-date. With the project feature backlog acting as a guide for the direction of the project and for helping in the decisions on what to put into which iteration, in combination it is a powerful tool. Students can benefit greatly at least by making themselves aware of the effort required and the effort actually put in.

Let's take a look at day 4 to see how things have changed. The noticeable change is the effort put in on day 4 which is more than anticipated. If you look at the last column in the table, 'Actual effort per task' you will see that the 'Review project scope' task has exceeded its estimated effort, which was two hours. The actual effort thus far for that one task is three hours. This means that when it comes to future iterations and the scope must be considered, we can refer back to the actual effort on this task and next time allow more time to conduct the scope review.

The student has put in five hours' effort on day 4 because there are no classes to attend on that Thursday. It's an opportunity to catch up

Iteration 1	3rd Oct 2016 - 16th Oct 2016				Week 1					Week 2					Actual effort per task
User Story/ Requirement / Feature / Deliverable	Task	Priority	Task ID	Estimate Effort hours	Mon	Tues	Wed	Thur	Fri	Mon	Tues	Wed	Thur	Fri	
1. Iteration Planning	Plan with supervisor/customer	Must	1.1	1	0.5	0	0	0	0	0	0	0	0	0	0.5
	Detailed planning on own	Must	1.2	2	1	1	0	0	0	0	0	0	0	0	2
2. Project Scope Analysis	Determine project scope	Must	2.1	6	0	2	2	2	0	0	0	0	0	0	6
	Customer analysis	Must	2.2	4	0	0	0	0	0	0	0	0	0	0	0
	Competitor analysis	Should	2.3	2	0	0	0	1	0	0	0	0	0	0	1
	Review project scope	Must	2.4	2	0	0	2	1	0	0	0	0	0	0	3
	Examine high likelihood risks	Should	2.5	1	0	0	0	0	0	0	0	0	0	0	0
	Review options for decisions	Should	2.6	1	0	0	0	1	0	0	0	0	0	0	1
3. Brief	Write Report Brief	Must	3.1	6	0	0	0	1	0	0	0	0	0	0	1
4. Iteration Review	Quality Review	Must	4.1	4	0	0	0	0	0	0	0	0	0	0	0
	Sign off	Must	4.2	1	0	0	0	0	0	0	0	0	0	0	0
	Review iteration	Must	4.3	2	0	0	0	0	0	0	0	0	3	0	0
	Ideal - remaining work effort in Ideal hours			32	29	26	22	19	16	13	10	6	3	0	
	Actual - remaining effort in Ideal hours			32	30.5	27.5	23.5	18.5	18.5	18.5	18.5	18.5	18.5	18.5	

Figure 3.6. Day 4 feature list

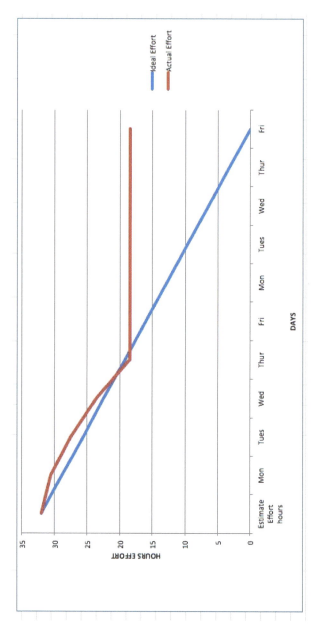

Figure 3.7. Day 4 burndown

on the project work and to put a bit more time in for when the days come where there is less time, such as when assignments from other modules are due to be submitted.

How has this affected the burndown? Let's look in figure 3.7. As can be seen, the actual effort on day 4 crosses the ideal effort line. This, as explained above, is because the student has put in 5 hours work on day 4, added to four hours on day three, Wednesday. So in two days, nine hours effort has gone into the project. The student wanted to make a real dent into the progress. It's clear the burndown is most expressive as an indicator of such progress. As it has been said above, we cannot automatically correlate hours worked with the quality of the project but it is certainly the case that more careful effort ought to result in a better product and deliverable for the university to mark.

Moving on through to the sixth day, we can see that an incredible surge has occurred in getting the iteration not only on schedule but its tasks completed early. The student has informed the supervisor that it may not be possible to put much effort into the iteration on days 7, 8 and 9 because of another commitment to submit an assignment due on day 9 of this iteration. This is a regular occurrence on projects and it is really important that this level of communication occur between student and supervisor, and student and customer. Why is this? First and foremost, the supervisor can be confident that the student is taking the project seriously and the relationship with his supervisor also seriously. So when it comes to understanding what can and cannot

Iteration 1 3rd Oct 2016 - 16th Oct 2016					Week 1					Week 2					Actual effort per task
User Story/ Requirement / Feature / Deliverable	Task	Priority	Task ID	Estimate Effort hours	Mon	Tues	Wed	Thur	Fri	Mon	Tues	Wed	Thur	Fri	
1. Iteration Planning	Plan with supervisor/customer	Must	1.1	1	0.5	0	0	0	0	0	0	0	0	0	0.5
	Detailed planning on own	Must	1.2	2	1	1	0	0	0	0	0	0	0	0	2
2. Project Scope Analysis	Determine project scope	Must	2.1	6	0	2	2	2	1	2	0	0	0	0	9
	Customer analysis	Must	2.2	4	0	0	0	0	1	0.5	0	0	0	0	1.5
	Competitor analysis	Should	2.3	2	0	0	0	1	2	0	0	0	0	0	3
	Review project scope	Must	2.4	2	0	0	2	1	1	0	0	0	0	0	4
	Examine high likelihood risks	Should	2.5	1	0	0	0	0	0	1	0	0	0	0	1
	Review options for decisions	Should	2.6	1	0	0	0	0	0	1	0	0	0	0	1
3. Brief	Write Report Brief	Must	3.1	6	0	0	0	1	2	0	0	0	0	0	3
4. Iteration Review	Quality Review	Must	4.1	4	0	0	0	0	0	0	0	0	0	0	0
	Sign off	Must	4.2	1	0	0	0	0	0	0	0	0	0	0	0
	Review iteration	Must	4.3	2	0	0	0	0	0	0	0	0	0	0	0
Ideal - remaining work effort in Ideal hours				32	29	26	22	19	16	13	10	6	3	0	
Actual - remaining effort in Ideal hours				32	30.5	27.5	23.5	18.5	11.5	7	7	7	7	7	

Figure 3.8. Day 6 feature list

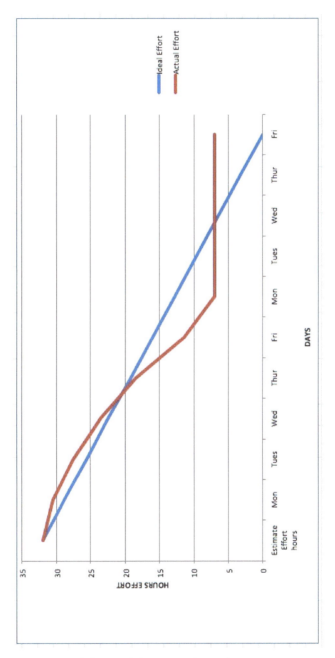

Figure 3.9. Day 6 burndown

be done, the supervisor understands the situation immediately. Let's view the burndown on day 6 in figure 3.9.

As can be seen, the actual effort is well ahead of the ideal and is visually **below** the ideal line in the figure. This means more work has been done by the student than the three hours per day average. This is time saved for when there is going to be very little work during the next two days as can be seen in figure 3.10.

In the iteration feature list, only one hour has been managed from day 6 to day 8 –two days of almost no project work. This is actually one hour more than expected and this is good news because it shows great commitment to the project from the student. From the supervisor's perspective, it shows the student is taking the project seriously, as it should be. These two days of barely any work done on the project are reflected in figure 3.11, the burndown chart up to and including day 8.

The student is still six hours short of the iteration target of 32 hours. Given the student has said that day nine is also going to be engaged on submitting another assignment, this leaves six hours for the last day. It is possible to do but a lot of work for the student who has some hours scheduled in labs that day also. If the student wants to continue on the weekend, this is also fine. Just because the iteration table says Monday to Friday, if the best working days for the student are Saturday and Sunday, then it's expected the student will change the iteration feature

Iteration 1	3rd Oct 2016 - 16th Oct 2016				Week 1					Week 2					Actual effort per task
User Story / Requirement / Feature / Deliverable	Task	Priority	Task ID	Estimate Effort hours	Mon	Tues	Wed	Thur	Fri	Mon	Tues	Wed	Thur	Fri	
1. Iteration Planning	Plan with supervisor/customer	Must	1.1	1	0.5	0	0	0	0	0	0	0	0	0	0.5
	Detailed planning on own	Must	1.2	2	1	1	0	0	0	0	0	0	0	0	2
2. Project Scope Analysis	Determine project scope	Must	2.1	6	0	0	2	2	1	2	0	0	0	0	9
	Customer analysis	Must	2.2	4	0	0	0	0	1	0.5	0	0	0	0	1.5
	Competitor analysis	Should	2.3	2	0	0	0	0	2	0	0	0	0	0	3
	Review project scope	Must	2.4	2	0	0	2	1	1	0	0	0	0	0	4
	Examine high likelihood risks	Should	2.5	1	0	0	0	0	0	1	0	0	0	0	1
	Review options for decisions	Should	2.6	1	0	0	0	0	0	1	0	0	0	0	1
3. Brief	Write Report Brief	Must	3.1	6	0	0	0	1	2	0	0	0	0	0	3
4. Iteration Review	Quality Review	Must	4.1	4	0	0	0	0	0	0	1	0	0	0	1
	Sign off	Must	4.2	1	0	0	0	0	0	0	0	0	0	0	0
	Review iteration	Must	4.3	2	0	0	0	0	0	0	0	0	0	0	0
Ideal - remaining work effort in Ideal hours				32	29	26	22	19	16	13	10	6	3	0	
Actual - remaining effort in Ideal hours				32	30.5	27.5	23.5	18.5	11.5	7	6	6	6	6	

Figure 3.10. Day 8 feature list

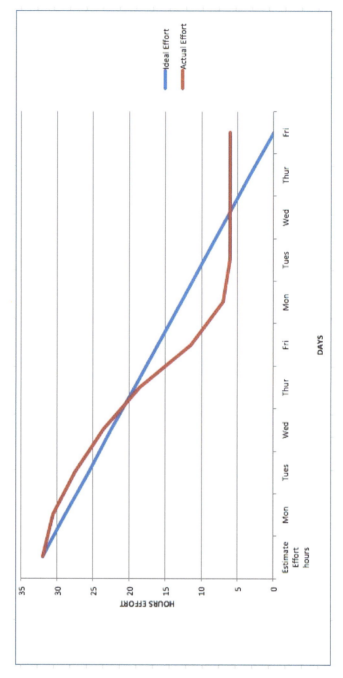

Figure 3.11. Day 8 burndown

Iteration 1 — 3rd Oct 2016 – 16th Oct 2016

User Story/Requirement/Feature/Deliverable	Task	Priority	Task ID	Estimate Effort hours	Week 1 Mon	Week 1 Tues	Week 1 Wed	Week 1 Thur	Week 1 Fri	Week 2 Mon	Week 2 Tues	Week 2 Wed	Week 2 Thur	Week 2 Fri	Actual effort per task
1. Iteration Planning	Plan with supervisor/customer	Must	1.1	1	0.5	0	0	0	0	0	0	0	0	0	0.5
	Detailed planning on own	Must	1.2	2	1	1	0	0	0	0	0	0	0	0	2
2. Project Scope Analysis	Determine project scope	Must	2.1	6	0	2	2	2	1	2	0	0	0	0	9
	Customer analysis	Must	2.2	4	0	0	0	0	1	0.5	0	0	0	0	1.5
	Competitor analysis	Should	2.3	2	0	0	0	1	2	0	0	0	0	0	3
	Review project scope	Must	2.4	2	0	0	2	1	1	0	0	0	0	0	4
	Examine high likelihood risks	Should	2.5	1	0	0	0	0	0	1	0	0	0	0	1
	Review options for decisions	Should	2.6	1	0	0	0	1	0	0	0	0	0	0	1
3. Brief	Write Report Brief	Must	3.1	6	0	0	0	0	2	1	0	0	0	1	4
4. Iteration Review	Quality Review	Must	4.1	4	0	0	0	0	0	0	1	0	0	0	1
	Sign off	Must	4.2	1	0	0	0	0	0	0	0	0	0	1	1
	Review iteration	Must	4.3	2	0	0	0	0	0	0	0	0	0	1	1
Ideal – remaining work effort in Ideal hours				32	29	26	22	19	16	13	10	6	3	0	
Actual – remaining effort in Ideal hours				32	30.5	27.5	23.5	18.5	11.5	7	6	6	6	3	

Figure 3.12. Day 10 feature list (end of iteration)

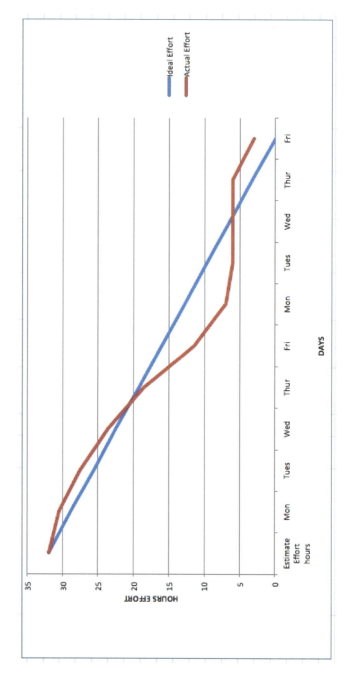

Figure 3.13. Day 10 burndown for completed iteration

list to reflect this and can remove two days such as Tuesday and Friday from the project schedule because these are the busy days in the classroom. The point is that the student and supervisor should be flexible. It's important to maintain a 10-day iteration but what days are project days does not really matter provided the labels on the table and graph reflect the reality. Let's close this two-day review with the final iteration feature list table and the burndown after the ten days are done, as shown in Figures 3.12 and 3.13.

Unsurprisingly, no effort went into day 9 but three hours effort went into day 10, which means the student fell only three hours short of the ideal effort for the iteration. Overall, 29 hours work went into what was anticipated to be a 32-hour iteration.

It is a good effort by the student and what is important on the final day is that two hours were spent in review with the goal of ensuring that the quality of work is of a good level from the outset. It does not mean that the quality is perfect, but the fact that the student is putting time and effort into improving quality in each iteration is a really beneficial part of this approach.

It's important to state here that it is not expected of the student to submit these files every two days to the supervisor. I've shown this here solely to demonstrate the approach. If the student does wish to point something out to the supervisor or has a question on what to do immediately next, then the iteration feature list is a great place to hold

ID	Feature / Task / Deliverable	Priority	Planned Iteration	Actual Iteration	Total Planned Effort	Total Actual Effort	Complete?	Issues / Log
1	Iteration Planning	Must	1	1	3	2.5	Y	Not sure if really makes sense.
2	Project Scope Analysis	Must	1	1	16	19.5	N	Don't know when to stop! Review in iteration 4
3	Project Brief Report	Must	1	1	6	4	Y	Don't need to add solutions yet! Thought I did.
4	Iteration Review	Must	1	1	7	3	Y	How do I test a document? Read for errors.
1	Iteration Planning	Must	2		3	0	N	
6	Interview Customers	Must	2		18	0	N	
7	Project Proposal Report	Must	2		8	0	N	
5	Iteration Review	Must	2		3	0	N	
	Analysis of Interviews with Customer	Must	3					
	User stories and requirements document	Must	3,4					
	Project Scope Analysis	Must	4					
	Strategic Modelling	Should	4					
	Data models	Must	5					
	Prototypes	Must	3 through 10					
	C# ASP.Net	Must	3 though 11					
	SQL database?	Should	?					
	Mobile version required?	Could	?					
	Examiner's report	Must	11, 12					

Figure 3.14. Project feature backlog end of iteration 1

that conversation around. And as it is an Excel file, it's easy to email the supervisor with the current status. Normally a supervisor ought to see each iteration table, planned and actual, and also check progress five days in. If we take a look at the project feature backlog we can see where we are after iteration one, and what may be required for iteration two (figure 3.14). As can be seen see, one of the activities planned for iteration 1, project scope analysis took longer than planned and is not complete. We've scheduled another look in approximately iteration 4. Why not iteration 2? This is because it is going to take 2-3 iterations to get a better understanding of the customer's requirements; at this point the student will be in a position to review the scope again. If is happens that iteration 3 is preferable (the student will know after iteration 2), then it's fine to bring the scope analysis forwards to iteration 3. A lot less time went into the iteration review than planned but enough was done to satisfy the student and supervisor that the right quality and the right direction are being followed. It's a task where the supervisor gets involved. The student did get an hour with the supervisor to discuss the iteration.

The single most important project activity in iteration two is the interviews the student plans to conduct with her customer. The allocation of 18 hours is roughly calculated on the number of interviews needed, and their analysis.[5] There's planning the interviews

---

[5] The book *Strategic Requirements Analysis*, Routledge, 2015, by myself describes how to plan, run, analyse and document interview findings.

(determining questions, locations, who is being interviewed), hours of interview (allocate one hour per interviewee), transcription, analysis, summary, extraction of potential user stories and requirements, and feedback, all of which should be recorded as separate line items in the iteration feature list for iteration 2. So when decomposing the interview customer task, it's now much easier to see where those 18 hours of allocated effort have come from. 18 hours may be an underestimate but it's good to find out.

So that is an iteration. Quite a bit of thought has gone into breaking tasks into smaller ones in order to estimate effort; the actual effort recorded can be used to plan later iterations. I trust it is clear how to use the tool, both for iterations and for the project. It's such a powerful way to track progress and to plan what needs to be done most.

Recording the plan

The student can cut and paste the completed project feature backlog as a project management document to submit with the remaining project documents. Each completed iteration feature list and burndown chart should also be cut and paste straight into the report. It makes for an excellent record of progress, a powerful tool for discussion of the project's activities and progress for the final project report and a great way for students to remember what they did and when. Comments on issues needed to be overcome and how this was done (replacing a project log book) are part of the project feature backlog.

As a tool for monitoring progress on a student project, the burndown is excellent. The spreadsheet automatically updates the burndown making it even easier to use. It's a good document to send to the supervisor on a weekly or bi-weekly basis to show progress. As previously said, the burndown and feature lists, if used honestly, also provide the student with an excellent view of her own progress.

Honesty: key to success

The student must be honest in logging the hours put in. The only person he is otherwise fooling is himself. When it comes to estimating how long each task will take, again an honest appraisal is needed. Initially, the estimate may be wildly different from the actual. This is fine so long as the next iteration takes this into account. If the amount of effort was severely underestimated then fewer tasks should be scheduled next iteration assuming similar tasks. If, on the other hand, the tasks are completed more rapidly than expected and to the satisfaction of the customer and supervisor, then more tasks can be added in the next iteration, assuming some degree of similarity. Given there is going to be a maximum of twelve iterations if we take bi-weekly durations, that is, ten working days per iteration, then the effort estimates may stabilise dramatically. Using prior knowledge to estimate current tasks is vitally important: A student will begin to see the scope of the project change as it progresses and will much less likely be caught out. My students are estimating to within one hour accuracy after having completed between four and five iterations. As described in the previous chapter, it is less easy to reliably track progress when you are in a project using the Gantt chart, be it big blocks or even fine-grained detail, simply because you cannot slip the delivery date on the individual project and you would need to re-plan the entire project each time you fall behind schedule.

Again, honesty is the key. A student can honestly reflect upon the effort put in and use the examiner's report to record impressions on why this is the case. These impressions, fresh in the memory, form the basis of the examiner's report with all its reflection. The student can even write the examiner's report as he or she progresses, beginning in iteration one.

The decision on what tasks or user stories or requirements or documents to work on should be made at the start of each 10-day cycle. The supervisor, especially at the start of the project, needs to be guiding the student as much as possible in what to do. On a traditionally planned project, the student often struggles to get going because he is uncertain where to begin. With the iterative plan, it is very clear, the student can get on with the work with some certainty and momentum.

Balanced Activity

It is very important that students get on with the actual project work as soon as they can, so from day 1 would be ideal. Of course, it will take time for a student to really get going but here the iterative approach can help. It's designed to best function when a set of different tasks are underway quickly, including programming. Estimation works best when there's prior similar experience. A supervisor should push the student to get going in an agile development approach and not just in planning. There's little point in using this iterative planning tool when each iteration consists of a single task like 'research' or 'design'. We are back to the big blocks Gantt chart and that is not going to help anyone. Some tasks will be high priority and some will not. But a balanced diet really helps in using the approach and in building the student's confidence and momentum. If a prototype is needed in the project, get the student working on a technical (code) aspect of it by the second iteration at the latest. Room is left for 'research' (finding immediate answers to technical questions), designing what is needed for that technical aspect – and no more than that. User stories and/or requirements determine the workings and rationale for that technical aspect. So the student may need to spend some time working with the customer and / or supervisor in producing the user story and any supporting documentation to go with it about its impact, who is affected and so on. These could be contextual models like business process diagrams or interview analysis or workflow or whatever is required. The point is to keep to a varied diet so that key deliverables – the Must Haves – receive the attention they deserve but not to block out all other activity. When the student has a complete user story done, he can estimate the next one from how long this one took. Any design work needed can also be a guide for estimating the next design work. The actual time taken to code one screen or to produce a mock-up from wireframes can be used to estimate the effort needed for the next screen mock up or functioning prototype.

If the big blocks or even detailed waterfall approach is embedded into the iterative approach, it will destroy the purpose of the iterative approach and render it next to useless. The next chapter compares an iteration against the Gantt chart approach in more detail. For now, concluding, the benefits of the two-week iterative approach are:

- The student can immediately see that work has been done and progress is being made, breeding confidence.
- The supervisor is in a like position.
- Stock can be taken of progress very early into the project because a key task in each cycle is to review progress and ensure the right quality is in place from the beginning.

If it looks like a key early part of the project has not been addressed sufficiently, then the two-week iteration will help in flagging this, simply by having a built-in review stage, and the missed activity can be scheduled in the next two-week cycle.

A word on scope

Scope refers mostly to the task of knowing what should be delivered as functionality and documentation, what does not need to be done and on keeping track of project changes throughout. Looking long term, it soon becomes clear whether the project's initial scope is too big or small. Ensuring that scope is being looked after means that the decision on when to start coding – if coding is a part of the project – can commence will be accurate. I personally recommend students commence coding as soon into a project as possible, as I said above. First, their skills are often rusty. Second, they may need to confirm understanding with a customer rapidly so a quick functional prototype may be the best way to do that. Third, the iterative approach is designed to do just this; that is, to work as fast as possible towards delivering quality functioning software to the customer.

The ten-day cycle of the iterative approach is an excellent way to keep track of scope. It soon becomes obvious where key functions or deliverables are at threat of not being delivered, simply because progress is so well monitored. Students can at this point, if needs be, relegate deliverables or functions deemed less important in iterations to focus on the Must Haves, that really do matter.

Estimating effort

Estimation has been discussed above but it is so vital to good project control in this agile approach that it warrants another discussion. Estimation is perhaps the trickiest part of planning. Traditional textbook estimation contains formulae and complexity that are not required for a student project. The agile way, perhaps described best in Extreme Programming[6], is to use an analogy called 'Yesterday's Weather'. This means that when a developer looks at a specific feature or a user story to code or a designer looks at a particular aspect of design to work on, in order to get an optimistic estimate of how long it will take to build, he will look at previous iterations of recorded actual effort. From here, the developer will compare the task, and if similar enough will simply take the last actual time to do the work as the estimate for the new work. Even if there are differences in the task, it's still important to estimate based on that actual – add another hour or two if the differences appear significant. This is a most excellent way to estimate effort and I encourage readers to look at Kent Beck and Martin Fowler's fabulous book in more detail.

For students, there will not likely be previous projects to look at. So the first couple of iteration's effort estimates have to be guided by the supervisor. If the supervisor has prior student project effort data – from previous years – it may be possible to get a general idea from this. But each student works at his own pace as does each developer. So other people's work would really only be a very rough ballpark figure.

---

[6] Kent Beck and Martin Fowler, Planning Extreme Programming, Addison-Wesley, 2001.

The first iteration is inevitably going to find the estimates fairly inaccurate. This is not a problem because the next iteration's estimates will be revised in accordance to the actual effort that was needed to complete the first deliverable or task.

Provided the student keeps to an average of 16 hours per week, it would be a very good start. If the project requires documentation rather than code, say a set of detailed business process models, then estimate how long each task in the following list takes for the first business process to elicit, draft, review, re-design, and get approval of, then record the actual effort per step and re-estimate the next business process according to the actual. Do this for all planned processes and you have a good estimate for the major deliverable of the project. You then can ask: is the project scope too small, too big? Is the complexity of the project too much, too simple? What can I introduce to boost the deliverable? What could be removed?

Do you change effort estimates in the middle of an iteration? No, is the short answer. If you are producing results far more quickly than the estimates, then add another task or two into the iteration, provided that quality control is still in place and conducted. If you are working more slowly, the next iteration assign less tasks, though you should speed up as you go through the project.

Estimation should become more accurate as the student progresses and this guides the ever-changing scope of the final deliverables. The number of requirements or features to be delivered is estimated, remember, but the quality should never be put into question.

It is key for supervisors to give good advice especially early in the project on how long they think tasks will take. This should be based upon prior experience. Of course, this is very rough estimate but it does come from someone who knows the project process.

Another word on the topic of literature reviews

Computing projects should deliver computer project-oriented deliverables rather than in-depth literature. There are exceptions, of course, but be wary of doing a literature review. In a typical masters computing project, a literature review should not be a part of the submission at all. Only in the examiner's report should any literature be introduced to support the discussion, if, and only if, it is required. If students deliver a long chapter entitled 'literature review', they have wasted a lot of time on their project – check your university's requirements carefully.

Prioritisation

What should a student do first in any iteration? This is not that difficult because most student projects revolve around exploration to begin with, then focus on producing a software product, be it a working prototype, an ecommerce website, an app or a functioning system. The key features of that software may already be known. It is really unlikely that students will dive into code immediately. The first iteration is mostly about investigating what the project involves but I do encourage students to get to coding as fast as possible. Why? Because balanced iterations accrue, complex requirements are worked out, programming experience is gained and the quality of the software deliverable is higher the more time is spent on the code. Here I assume a correct understanding of the requirements, having worked with the customer to elicit and understand their context and meaning.

At my university my experience, which I presume is not entirely unique, is that many students spend the first three-to-four weeks of the project working out who their supervisor is and working out only vaguely what their project may be. This is four weeks completely wasted. That's one third of semester one effectively down the drain. Of course, not all projects are like this and many students have produced masses of work by that point. There's also an interim planning report deliverable and this needs to be submitted, marked and a viva held to give the student a Go / No Go decision and some advice. I like this idea but it comes far too late in the project schedule – the deadline for the viva is usually the last day before Christmas holidays begin for students, meaning virtually no work may have been done by Christmas other than in getting to this stage gate. The focus is wrong because it gives the student the impression that the project can more or less wait until semester two starts. This interim stage gate should occur much earlier – four-to-six weeks maximum into semester 1.

Students should be given a deadline of finding a supervisor within one week of semester 1 and the project should commence immediately, with a proposal submitted after the first iteration. The interim report – if one is needed at all – should come at the end of iteration 2. If universities want students to produce great projects, they have to treat the project as a professional engagement and expect the student's attitude and effort to match.

Prioritizing with MoSCoW

All tasks, whatever they may be, should be prioritised. The general rule of thumb is to aim for 50-60 per cent 'must have' tasks and the remainder 'should' and 'could' haves. The idea behind this is driven by the fact that the project's duration will not go beyond the set deadline and it is vital to deliver to the customer/supervisor that which is vital. The should and could have tasks are the student's contingency in each iteration. If a Must Have overruns its estimate and it really must be done in this iteration, then the student can eat into the time allocated for should and could have tasks. This means that no float (a traditional planning calculation used to work out the critical path through a project) is needed. Simply use the could/should have time allocated to complete the must have. If there is some opportunity to deliver more than the must have features or requirements then that is good; deliver the should and could have features allocated to that iteration also, dependent upon the time left in that specific iteration. Each iteration should decide what must have features / tasks are worked on. Here's what the MoSCoW priorities mean:

- Must Have
    - Imperative now; business / project cannot go on without it.
- Should Have
    - Will cause workarounds if we don't have but can live without.
    - Document the workarounds.
- Could Have
    - Would be nice to have at some point – may be important soon, before the project deadline.
- Won't Haves
    - Don't need in the time frame of the project and probably not for some time afterwards.

A supervisor may ask the student why every feature needs to be must have, could have or should have. Why is every feature needed? The student when working with a customer should take the view that each feature is a won't have until the customer explains and justifies why it must be included or why it is a could or should have. This open discussion gets both parties thinking more deeply about the real needs of the project and product than the superficial glance each may initially receive, and will put the student on course much more quickly in producing the right product. Be aware, though, that priorities can change and this should be taken on board. If a customer's business need changes, then its IT solution may change with it.

Quality

Quality is the key to a good project. A project doesn't always have to have covered enormous ground to get a good mark provided the quality of the project is high. An iterative approach all but guarantees higher quality than the Gantt chart approach because each iteration contains a planning phase at its start and a review phase at its end. This means that there are regular checks on progress and deliverables. Quality checking in agile includes automated testing. A student project is unlikely to have that opportunity but quality can be delivered in other ways. For instance, when a user story or requirement is written, the student should write a way to test it before attempting to code it. This will afford the student the opportunity to ask questions: what does this user story really mean? What result should I get from this function? What is really going to trigger it? Are there pre-requisites for this function to operate, such as whether I have an account with this company prior to accessing its full list of features and products? Students can ask about data: what specific items of data need to be captured and retrieved? What exactly do I need to alter in the data model to ensure this specific user story will work? For missing items or for clarity, the student should talk to the customer – it's the customer's story. If there is no customer, talk the user story through with the supervisor.

For a two-week iteration, you would probably spend day one planning in detail. (Which is really 3 hours effort given the 16 hours per week dedicated to the project – as a rule of thumb.) Day 10 should be spent reviewing the result of the previous 8 days (day 1 is spent on planning) of analysis / design / coding, testing or writing documents. (Which is really three hours' effort.) Note that it isn't imperative for students to work Monday-Friday or to put in only 3 hours on any day. I have students who work most on Saturday where 5 hours or more effort may be put into the project. Some students try to get 16 hours work done in just two days because of lectures and labs they need to attend and often because of part-time work commitments. Provided about 32 hours' effort goes into the project over a two-week period, it isn't important which day it occurs or for how long. However, students must commit to the project and the effort required in each iteration if this approach is to be of any value.

Risk

Risk is reduced because of the on-going cycle of iteration planning and review. Part of the planning and reviewing phases should think about any risks to the work planned for that iteration. Risk is rarely a driving factor for a student project but note of the key risks should occur. These risks need to be reviewed every iteration. It's only a few minutes every two weeks.

You can ask questions about each feature: What's the risk to this feature being delivered? Well, a review of scope, or the coding of an early user story, may actually take a lot longer than imagined, for one. So mitigate not by dedicating a whole iteration to it but by allowing the next iteration to contain an element of time for the task if, and only if, it is not completed and is vital.

Students need to define between business risk – in the hands of the customer / supervisor – and technical risk: in the hands of the student, or university if a website is meant to be housed on the university server but that server is entirely unreliable. If the customer's business changes direction half-way through a project, this will dramatically affect the project. The student needs to know how (different user stories; already programmed features no longer relevant, etcetera), and to discuss with the customer what this means. It's important the student can complete the project even if it is then done without the customer. A customer has to also commit to the project in recognising the student must produce deliverables the university needs, and not solely those required by the customer. In the rare cases where a customer went out of business mid-way through a project, students have still completed but with me in the customer role as well as supervisor. If the customer drops the project because it is unimportant, a low priority, then it earns a loss of reputation with the student and the university, and this is bad for business so it is in the customer's interest to facilitate a good project environment for the student. It's a rare occurrence but when it has occurred, I have not had a student left high and dry.

Technical risks are in the hands of the student (unless the university is at fault). Technical risks are those risks around the project's products – designs, code, documentation. If a student takes on a complex programming project but cannot programme to the level required, what then needs to happen is to either change the focus of the project or reduce the programming difficulty. The supervisor is invaluable in discussing these risks and how to resolve them. Many is the time I have had to guide students in reducing their coding ambition of delivering a full functioning product in live use to one of a detailed and great to use prototype. Sometimes re-scoping is needed because the student does not have the skill set or because the project's hard deadline is looming.

Do we need a risk register? Or a risk log? Do we need to record risks to the level of Prince2? No, not really. Why not? For one, the risk register will not be kept up to date. Secondly, risk is managed during planning and during review. Each task, when planned, needs a thirty second risk appraisal: any foreseeable problems? Yes / No? Yes – well, what are they? What do we do now? No – ok, next feature / item of work. Any issues around risk worth making a note of can go into the project feature backlog issue column. This way, any issues or risks are immediately tied to the plan of action at the time of asking.

Quality and risk for 3rd party customer

Quality is enhanced and risk reduced respectively because the student can plan and get feedback from the customer in these two-weekly cycles. The customer will know when other priorities are occurring (such as other assignment deadlines) and so not expect much during these times. Even though not much is happening, because the customer is aware of this, there is less pressure on the student.

The customer must be active in the planning – deciding what will be developed assuming the project is delivering a product for the customer. The customer should be responsible for selecting the user stories / requirements and for clarifying them with the student. The customer must also be active in the review phase to approve work done or at least recommend what should be done next, as and when appropriate, especially when code is involved. The earlier the customer is engaged in viewing results like screens or process models or functioning code – whatever it is – the more likely the project is viewed as a success in the customer's eyes. This is because the customer can direct the student to the right level of quality, in correcting any misunderstandings about business requirements or context, and ensure the documents and / or software are the right look and feel for the customer's business. The student should schedule a day every iteration to be on location with the customer, preferably one day per week. That close contact works wonders in getting the product done the way the customer needs it. The customer is also aware through this closer contact of the student's university requirements.

No log book required

Traditionally, when a student wrote up the documentation for her project, it was important to keep a log book for notes on daily activities, experiences, issues and resolutions. The whole schedule of the project can be planned in terms of iterations and these include days of inactivity where the planned velocity is 'zero' because of assignments / exams / classes / projects / holidays. Just add comments to the 'Log – Issues' column in the project feature backlog or write on the spreadsheet of every iteration what the problems and achievements were for that moment, and how they were resolved or came about. The specifics of the work are already there in terms of activities and effort. Cut and paste direct into the final report.

Summary: Embrace the New Way

Just about everything in traditional project management is heavyweight and not fit for purpose for a typical student computing project. So a new way is needed. Using the three interlinked tools of the project feature backlog, iteration feature list and burndown chart, pretty much all management is handled on a single person student project. The fact that the tool is in Excel means it is easy to keep up to date and it's easy to keep the supervisor up to date also. If there is a customer, he should decide with the student in terms of features etcetera what will go into each iteration and this must be relayed to the supervisor. As it is an Excel file, it is easy! Just an email.

How does this agile approach really stack up against the waterfall Gantt chart? The next chapter compares these planning tools.

CHAPTER 4: COMPARING THE TWO

The book has thus far discussed the weaknesses of traditional project planning and the strengths of agile planning. Lest this be considered unfair, this chapter will compare the two planning documents, one a two-week slot of the Gantt chart presented in figure 2.1 against a 10-day iteration feature list as was discussed in chapter 3. So in effect, this would be figures 3.12 – 3.14, the iteration feature list, the burndown and the project feature backlog for the two-week completed iteration. Please turn back to review these three figures. Compare against a two-week block of the Gantt chart shown in figure 4.1 below. My purpose is to highlight how each presents the student, supervisor and customer with what they need to know for the project to be successful.

As you should be able to see there is really no comparison. We still have the complete Gantt chart as shown earlier and have boxed in the first two weeks (figure 4.1). Irrespective of how we look at this figure, the project feature backlog is more detailed. You might say that this is unfair and the tasks in the project feature backlog should be included. OK, agreed. So let's compare again, replacing the original Gantt activities with those from the project feature backlog, first iteration. This section of the Gantt is highlighted in figure 4.2. Even with this enhancement, it is the iteration feature list that provides the real detail of each main task, including estimated effort and actual effort. Where is this recorded on the Gantt chart?

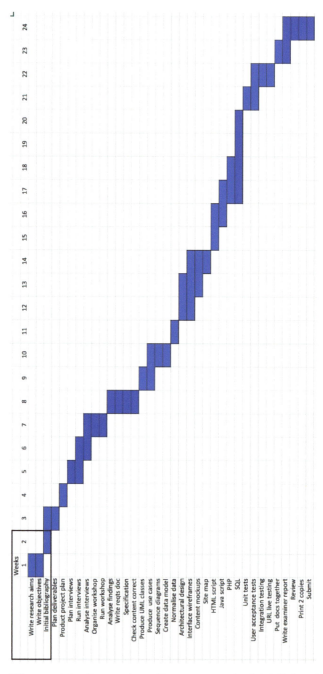

Figure 4.1. Gantt chart first two weeks highlighted

There are sophisticated Gantt chart tools on the market but do students get access to these tools? We have also discussed the fact that we must plan and review every two weeks in the iterative approach. This is still technically possible with a Gantt chart but you need to re-draw the entire chart each cycle and explicitly include the iteration planning and review activities (see figure 4.2). That would be time consuming to do. Perhaps there are tools to do this too?

Figure 4.2. Snapshot of Gantt chart

Yes, but again you need to ask, does the project deadline just slip? It would indeed once you've overrun an activity because the Gantt is dependency-based. A student does not have the luxury of a slipped submission deadline. So then the student has to either shorten the duration estimates on the Gantt or remove some activities. And then re-draw the entire chart. How can the student or the supervisor accurately estimate effort on code activities that are still months away from being addressed? What happens when the requirements change? Do we need to re-draw the entire Gantt? Where can we plot actual progress against planned? There are tools to do this but we have to keep re-drawing the Gantt to stop the schedule slipping. The focus is obsessively on the future and not on the now. The burndown shows us the now and only the now. The iteration feature list in fine detail plans for the now and whatever remains of the current two weeks. Then we take stock and start the next plan. The deadline cannot slip but the deliverables initially conceived can be reduced, or indeed increased, in scope. The customer can change her mind and the next iteration can cope with the change, indeed welcome it.

If you look at figure 4.2 there's overlap in tasks (iteration planning and project scope analysis occur at the same time according to the Gantt). It is possible to set up project planning tools to show daily activity. But do we keep all that information on one page? Where do we store actual effort? Can we easily review the previous iteration simply by clicking on the previous worksheet tab button on the spreadsheet to get our previous actuals to use as this iteration's estimates?

As the iteration progresses on a daily basis, the burndown chart visually shows how much effort is recorded in the iteration feature list. So you have both data and visuals. You can see which tasks are Must Have against lower priorities. Where is this visible on the Gantt chart?

Summary

This is a short chapter because the entire book has been about this comparison. But it is necessary to place one approach next to the other. Every time I look at a Gantt chart, though it can look impressive, I see wishful thinking and little relation to what is going to happen. The entire idea of traditional planning is to come up with what we would like to see, how we would like to work, but not how we actually do work. The agile approach presented, once through an iteration or two really does show how work is truly progressing and the planning of the next iteration should be around that actual work done, how the student actually works, at the student's actual pace. This is the difference: Gantt is an ideal and Agile is real.

CHAPTER 5:
THE CUSTOMER AND THE SUPERVISOR

This part of the book looks at what taking an agile approach to managing a student project means to the student's supervisor and any external customers for whom the product is being developed. Each will have expectations and responsibilities for a successful project. Let's start with the customer.

The Customer

Ultimately, the customer has to accept that the student is following a plan of action to get a degree. This means the customer realises there are deliverables that the student needs to put together of which the customer will have no interest in terms of the customer's business. Whether the customer accepts this approach taken to planning the project by the student depends upon the project and the customer's own project management approach. Engineering companies have less experience of agile because software is a smaller part of their business. So traditional planning is more often used. However, the student's job is to produce a software-oriented product even if it runs on hardware that the customer makes or uses specifically. There's no reason a student should change his approach unless the customer is insistent. But that puts the project under less control and opens the door for the many issues discussed above about traditional planning. It is the student's project process, not the customer's.

Assuming we have an agreeable customer, the fact that this iterative approach is taken should appeal to him. This is because the customer is engaged in the project at the planning and review stages of each iteration. Also the fact that the student aims to begin code development as soon as possible. This allows the customer to see results more quickly and can direct the student more closely to the must have deliverables the customer really needs. The customer should also provide the user stories and continue to do so throughout the project should new requirements emerge. The customer must prioritise the user stories and requirements. The customer should be directing which user story gets developed in the next iteration or at least accept what activity is conducted in which iteration. The student has to provide the technical work to ensure the user story will function, but not more than is needed to meet the user story or stories for that specific iteration.

It should be a win-win for the customer to see a student taking such an approach to the project because the customer and the student are much more engaged and communicating on a weekly basis. The quality of the student's work thus is likely to be higher and many risks reduced. The customer should be able to get the features he or she really needs because of this continual engagement throughout the project.

It's important the customer take the project and student seriously enough. It's possible the student will work on a mission critical project. I've had students work on a website for their customers that really did bring in 30 per cent more business as a result of the student project; this simply would not have happened without that student's effort. There's really little downside to this planning approach for the customer because everything is made clear by the longer view of the project feature backlog and the immediate iteration feature list and burndown.

The Supervisor

Much of the book has inevitably discussed the role of the supervisor so I have no wish to repeat myself unnecessarily. But there are some points worth making here.

First, the supervisor must know enough about agile planning to be able to give the necessary support to the student. If the student chooses to take an agile planning approach to her project, it behoves the supervisor to know something about it too. So supervisors, please read this book, and others, on agile planning. Supervisors really ought to know something about the student's subject area also. Some institutions will say that supervisors are there to guide the process only but this is old-fashioned thinking. The point of call that students have for their project is their supervisor. The supervisor should know quite a bit about the topic of the student's chosen subject. I don't imply the supervisor need know it all because there should be a department of colleagues with various areas of expertise that students can call upon. To take on a student project and know nothing of the topic is high risk for the student and a mechanism for disengaging from the project for the supervisor – because it is of little to no interest.

If you work on an IT project, a real one in a real company, you expect the project manager to know something about the project, the customer and perhaps one or two more technical aspects, or at least to be able to relate to it. If, as an employee, you are assigned a supervisor, someone more experienced in your role than you, to guide you in your early career, then you expect that supervisor to know something of your subject. Otherwise, how can you come to that person with the technical points you need clarity on? It's time universities caught up with the rest of the world in this regard. Supervise projects you know something about. There are exceptions where you may have an excellent student whose choice is programming but that student really would like your guidance on planning. I've supervised those projects and they work but for the odd occasion, almost weekly, when the student says: I can't solve this programming problem. I can't even give a rough idea in those circumstances. So the student has to call on another member of staff who isn't supervising that project and has to give extra time, which is given. So it's necessary students get a supervisor who knows something about the topic. University quality assurance has historically been based on due diligence to process but not product. It's there to protect the staff their blushes. Commercially this is a sure guarantee of failure. Given students are currently paying a fortune to study, it's about time universities (no names mentioned) caught up a bit with practice.

The supervisor, as said, has to know the planning approach laid out in this book. The student is likely to have had some exposure to agile and though he can get the instruction needed from this book alone, it really is vital that the supervisor has some idea too and this is especially so at the start of the project. Given the tool discussed in this book is downloadable and should be used by the student, it's key the supervisor learn the tool too. It's quite quick to learn and easy to use once you know it; but you have to also know something about agile development beyond a few catch phrases. It's another investment in time but I think it worth the effort judging by the results of my project students who have taken this approach to heart.

The basis for the agile planning approach is the two-weekly iteration. The idea behind a two-week schedule is that each two-week period is a mini-project in itself, at least in ideal (one week is too short to get a substantial amount of work done and four weeks is too long between planning and reviewing, and very difficult to plan for – it's getting into Gantt chart territory).

The ideal engagement model for the student with the supervisor is:

- A 30-minute planning session at the start of the iteration.
- A progress email / stand up meeting at the end of week 1 (10 minutes).
- A progress email / stand up meeting at the start of week 2 (10 minutes).

- A review meeting at the end of week 2 of 30 minutes.

This is an ideal situation and I realise the supervisor's timetable may not permit such flexibility. But so long as there is a regular meeting and one is to plan (first week), the other to review (second week), that's a good start.

What should supervisors do in meetings?

The above list states a 30-minute meeting is all the student will get. I put 30 minutes because this is what time allocation I get per student in my timetable. But thirty minutes at the beginning is not enough. A recent first meeting with a student, after several email rounds, lasted one and a half hours, to get the project idea more narrowly and concretely defined. Subsequent meetings were between 20 minutes and an hour. Later stand ups have been sometimes only 2 minutes. But that was all that was needed once we got through the first pangs of planning and adoption of the approach. If the supervisor, like me, has seven or so project students per year, that's three and half to four hours of student meetings, weekly. Plus emails, plus any follow ups and unplanned meetings. That's quite a bit of time. But one of the purposes of this agile approach is a far more satisfactory engagement model for supervisors.

There's a lot I can say here as a supervisor but the key points are around the same topics as those addressed earlier. The supervisor has to be honest with him or herself and put in the hours needed for the student. That's not always been done, talking about myself. But this new means of student engagement makes more sense to me as a supervisor and is of much greater value to my students. But the student must also make the effort to contact and engage the supervisor. Despite best efforts, every year a student does not do this. No matter how good the planning approach, it won't make a difference if the student does not reply to emails, call for or turn up to meetings.

In a student meeting, the supervisor should be able to guide the student in putting together the iterative feature list in the first couple of iterations. Post this, the student should be experienced and confident enough to put a plan together herself, then get the supervisor to validate it. I often ask my students why he or she has chosen, for example, a lot less effort for a programming task than the previous iteration. The reply typically does make sense: the previous iteration had to put the underlying architecture in place too. The current iteration just builds functions on top of it. So, I ask, why didn't you put 'architecture build' as a task in the last iteration list? Oops. The student forgot because it wasn't originally considered. Next time. You see how it goes? The student has to include such level of detail in the iterative plan in order to get a really accurate picture of the iteration. If another architecture build is required, knowing the actual effort it took last time would make the next easier to plan.

The supervisor should be able to check the plan and ensure there are enough non-critical activities, that is, those assigned as should and could haves, to allow for slippage when necessary. The supervisor should be confident enough to direct the student into careful thinking about priorities where there is no customer and even when there is a customer.

The supervisor should be in a position of understanding the technical things that the student needs to do (within reason) in order to review them. I am not a coder though I did teach C++ 19 years ago! So if a student's project is 85 per cent programming, how can I help in planning and review? I can review screens, and the basic documents, whatever they may be – designs, UML and so on. But the primary deliverable the student is working towards, software code, I am of no help at all in supervising and reviewing. Hence, it makes sense to have supervisors supervise projects they know something about. In this example, the planning documents may be brilliant but the code spaghetti – and I wouldn't know it. So as a supervisor in this case I'd view my role as failing the student.

The supervisor should be able to recommend that the student drop certain features from their project in order for them to focus on more critical ones. Again, knowledge of the topic is vital to be able to do this. The student needs reassurance of quality – is the work good enough for a 2:1 classification, for a 1st? How can I judge that if I know about business requirements but not about AI algorithms? It's really ridiculous to assume I can help the student in this critical regard when the student's project is all about complex code. The old order has changed – yield to the new!

The main role of the supervisor, other than marking the work, is to give the student confidence that he or she is doing the right project and doing it in the right way. Though this sounds somewhat less than technical and hands on, most of my students really need this boost. They need to know that they are producing the right products, the right documents and so on. For most students, the project is new ground. Sadly, as we tend to spoon-feed our students more and more, for them to be hit with the big project where the student does all the work, guidance is vital, direction is vital. Here the agile planning tools stand tall against the traditional Gantt approach. The agile tools presented in this book are both forward looking (project feature backlog) and immediate (iteration feature list and burndown chart). The supervisor can really help the student grow in confidence by working closely with him in putting the first iteration plans together, and in setting out the rough longer term deliverables and activities.

Supervisors also need to be firm (but still polite) in meetings when needed, when it is clear the student isn't engaging in the right way.

If the customer is demanding too much of the student or not engaging appropriately, it is the supervisor who needs to inform the student of what to do. It is also the supervisor who has to report such issues to the person who is in charge of running the student project module, to find out what to do about it.

Issues with the approach – there are issues! – and with supervising using this approach are discussed, with potential solutions, in the next chapter.

CHAPTER 6: ISSUES AND SOLUTIONS

No single approach to project management is perfect. Projects do not ever run perfectly. They can run well, even smoothly. Many do not. Every single student project I have supervised and marked has had problems to overcome. It is the same here. There are issues that need to be addressed if we are to take on the agile approach presented here with open eyes.

Students really need their supervisors to guide them in the use of the agile tool. The connection between the project feature backlog and the iteration feature list has had some of my students confused. They've put entirely unrelated activities into each. So I have learned to work a bit more in explaining what the project feature backlog means and how it relates to the iteration feature list. Hopefully this book has helped explain the differences.

Perhaps the biggest issue is to avoid over-planning. The tool and approach actually look quite complex compared to the Gantt chart. The effort needed to honestly maintain the actual effort taken is an effort. In my view, and those of students who have used the tool, a worthwhile effort, once they got the hang of it. The step up from a single or group project on another module to the actual project is a big step and students are often nervous at the beginning in defining their project, and then getting on with it. Add the planning tool to the equation and this has been seen as an extra thing to worry about. But, as ever, when the student puts the tool into use, he can see over the course of one, two or three iterations how valuable this tool is. It is a definite overhead in time to the student in taking on the Agile approach described here, especially at the start because he is just not used to planning. But as the project unfolds the agile approach becomes a powerful ally. It is important that the supervisor demand, politely, that the student plan and review on a bi-weekly basis in some detail what each day should, and actually did, entail. The Gantt chart, either depicting big block activities such as 'code entire interface of an e-commerce site' for 4 weeks, or the detailed Gantt breaking that work down into several smaller activities, no longer seem so terrifying. But I hope by now you will agree that the Gantt scheduling approach has too many pitfalls and is virtually useless in guiding you in what to do, because its focus is on what could be done rather than how work is actually done.

Something of importance that both the student and the supervisor must make note of and not lose sight of, is that if a student puts in 400 hours work on the project, and uses this tool to keep track of actual progress against planned progress, this does not necessarily mean the project will deserve a higher grade. Normally it does because the extra care the student puts in. It's difficult to do this when using the traditional planning approach. But let us please be clear: good work is still needed to get a good mark.

Is the agile approach suitable for all projects? Not necessarily. If the computing project has a majority hardware element to it where the software part is just a short phase, then I would recommend taking the traditional approach for the hardware development though the software part could still be agile. It's up to the student but often when the software aspect is a lot less effort than the hardware part, the student may be best advised to keep to the engineering approach, where Gantt may suit the situation more. However, be forewarned that traditional planning is really only focussed on a dependency approach and not on how students actually work.

Honesty has been discussed earlier and so I will not re-iterate what has previously been said. But honesty is the bedrock of this approach. Supervisors need to motivate students when their project appears to be going awry. The agile planning approach can help here by keeping the focus on the short-term, the now, rather than the longer view of when the submission needs to be handed in. Building on smaller successes, which suits the agile approach, really does grow confidence. This small steps approach – Kaizen – is typical of agile projects. Kaizen is beyond the scope of this book but I recommend readers go look it up.

Initial enthusiasm can wane for the agile approach as the student dives headlong into the project. Here the supervisor has to work to keep the student using the tool. It does take effort but the results are worth it. The supervisor will see the wane when the student forgets to send the iteration feature list for the next iteration. It's down to the supervisor to keep the student engaged in using this approach and maintaining the required professionalism throughout the project.

Obsession with planning and nothing but planning has not occurred in my experience but we could hypothesize that it might. The risk of becoming planning obsessive is that the project does not deliver a product but a set of extremely detailed plans. The supervisor needs to see concrete deliverables throughout the project. Again, the tool helps in this in that if it is used correctly, each iteration will deliver something the supervisor and customer should be able to review.

Let's hypothesize that the tool does not suit the project's needs but there are parts the student would still like to use. Again, this is hypothesis but let's flow with the go. If the student really only needs one or two aspects of the tool (such as just the iteration feature lists, or just the project feature backlog) because other elements were already in place or superseded, then go with what the student needs. Also, if a part of the tool may need redesigning, go ahead and redesign it. This is a free tool, not for sale or resale. But feel free to tailor it to your needs.

What if the student is aware of agile management and is keen to take on this approach, but the supervisor is either unaware or not keen? The student has to go with what works for him and not for the supervisor. It has to be the responsibility of the supervisor to learn the tool at least – to read this book and / or other agile management introductory books.

All along the emphasis of this book is on practical projects, not dissertations. Will the tool work with a dissertation-oriented project? Probably it won't work so well. A dissertation is primarily an essay-oriented project, with a substantial research and / or literature review section. This tool is really more for practical projects where something has to be built or designed or both, as opposed to essayed.

There may be more issues I have not considered because I have not encountered them. But if you do, don't panic, use the tool, amend the tool or if it really doesn't fit (which is likely for hardware projects that have minimal software activities) then use something else.

CHAPTER 7: SUMMARY

A summary is meant to be short because it is called a summary. So here we have a short summary. Not being a student, at least on the course I teach, from the way I look at student projects, and the experiences my students are having using the agile planning tool, they are much happier. There's a strong sense of workload, what is realistic, what is not. There's little guilt if a two-week iteration passed with virtually nothing done, so long as it is documented and the time is made up later. The fact that students can see for themselves real progress, or otherwise, only benefits them.

From a supervisor's perspective, I can comprehend not just in the final documentation what students did far more clearly than with a Gantt chart, but I can also feel happier about progress monitoring during the project. It is simply a lot easier to do with the backlog, feature list and burndown chart. There is a proviso that supervisors know what they are looking at when they see these tools. As this book is primarily aimed at computing projects, it is assumed supervisors should be aware of the Agile approach to projects, even if they are not especially familiar with the details.

Primarily though, communication is much improved between student and supervisor as the student can email progress rapidly via the Excel spreadsheet. The supervisor can instantaneously chart the student's progress. The supervisor has to make the effort also. So there's a balance: the student and supervisor work together to plan and review the two-week's work. The customer also must engage here too. He or she will feel far happier with this engagement model where the student gets to spend one day minimum every iteration on site at the customer's location, assuming timetables permit and the customer permits. Why wouldn't the customer permit this?

I spent much of this book talking about what doesn't work with traditional project management in the circumstance of an individual student computing project. I don't say 'never use waterfall / Gantt', but I suggest if you are about to embark on a year-long student project that is initially ill-defined in terms of requirements and / or deliverables, the quality of which is not necessarily dubious but again uncertain, then go with the Agile approach. Even if everything that needs to be built is crystal clear, go with the Agile approach anyway. It will deliver better results.

The current job market appreciates students who can work in an Agile environment. Many smaller companies, and indeed, larger ones, are embracing the 'new' Agile approach (it's been around quite some time now). So in terms of employability, students can only enhance their chances because Agile:

- reduces risk by on-going review and continual engagement with the customer, by prioritising and by sensible (evidential) estimation of effort from prior actual recorded effort –post iteration one;

- improves quality because it is inbuilt to plan, test and review in every two-week cycle;
- delivers working results because of its focus on getting the product right for the customer / supervisor in small manageable chunks;
- the tools presented are simple and easy to use – you just need Microsoft Excel and a bit of practice.

If the agile approach is applied well, it's a win-win for the student and supervisor.

ABOUT THE AUTHOR

Karl A. Cox, PhD, is a Senior Lecturer at the University of Brighton, in the School of Computing, Engineering and Mathematics. He has taught business-IT alignment and IT project management to undergraduates and postgraduates for close to 20 years and has published over 90 articles and book chapters on the subject of IT and business requirements, alignment, processes and project management. Karl has also consulted to companies in the UK, Australia and Japan. He owned a consulting business in Australia specialising in business-IT alignment and management consulting, and was a senior research scientist at NICTA, Ltd, in Australia. Whilst there, his focus was on the commercial development of methods to improve business-IT alignment, as well as conduct consulting and research engagements with companies across Australia and in Japan. Find out more: www.drkarlcox.com.

www.ingramcontent.com/pod-product-compliance
Lightning Source LLC
Chambersburg PA
CBHW041142050326
40689CB00001B/453